THE DESPISED POOR
Newburgh's War on Welfare

THE DESPISED POOR

Newburgh's War on Welfare

by Joseph P. Ritz

BEACON PRESS · BOSTON

To My Gentle Ann ——

　　　. . . A BIRTHDAY PRESENT

CONTENTS

ILLUSTRATIONS

INTRODUCTION

SINCE THE SUMMER OF 1961, Newburgh, New York, its welfare program, and its irrepressible City Manager, Joseph McDowell Mitchell, have been the subject of articles, cartoons, and editorials in publications ranging in size from *The Montana Citizen* to *Life,* and in political viewpoint from the right-wing *National Review* to the liberal *The Nation.* Religious magazines such as the Roman Catholic *Commonweal* and the Protestant *Christian Century* have added their voices to the discussion. Overseas, the controversy was aired in such diverse journals as *The Manchester Guardian* and *The London Sunday Express.* The National Broadcasting Company filmed an award-winning "White Paper" documentary on the city and its welfare issue, and CBS broadcast a similar program. For a time in the early sixties, it appeared as though the newsmen in Newburgh outnumbered the welfare recipients.

Now the battle has quieted. The squads of out-of-town reporters and the television crews have left. City Manager Mitchell, too, has left the community. And yet, for many, Newburgh remains a symbol. Only, people disagree on what that symbol represents.

Newburgh became a rallying cry for those who regard present welfare programs as weakening the moral fiber

of the nation. To those in the welfare field and their supporters, it is a reminder that the belief that the poor are
essentially unworthy and immoral is as old as debtors'
prisons and as widespread as poverty itself.

Conservatives use it as an example of a courageous fight
by a local government against federal and state "tyranny."
Liberals point to it as a lesson on how a community can
be held, for a time, in the power of a publicity-seeking
demagogue. It has been credited with bringing about a
change in state and federal welfare laws, and derided for
its failure to uncover chiselers or to cut its welfare budget.

Despite all that has been written and said about Newburgh in the past, many questions have not been completely
answered to everyone's satisfaction. This book is written
as a sincere effort to answer those questions.

That is one purpose. It is not the only one. Had Newburgh remained an ordinary small town, known to few
outside the Hudson Valley, the number of people on its
welfare rolls, the way they live, the racial makeup of its
population, the social philosophy of its City Manager, or
the politics of its City Council would be of little concern
outside its own community.

But, like Selma, Alabama, Newburgh both stirred national indignation and evoked national applause. And, like
Selma, it had an effect on future legislation. That, too, is
part of the Newburgh story. This book is partly the story,
also, of the mild-mannered man who brought forth so much
indignation and applause, Joseph McDowell Mitchell. Without Mitchell and his peculiar abilities to make headlines,
there might not have been a Newburgh controversy. And
it was he, like an actor who refuses to leave the stage after
his scene is over, who kept the national spotlight on the city
long after the program's end.

Reveille at Newburgh

Courtesy of Albany (N.Y.) *Knickerbocker News*

In the beginning, a great number of people and news media throughout the nation felt that Mitchell's get-tough welfare policy was the answer to a big problem.

Many people who today think of Newburgh only as a sea-food sauce remember Mitchell. Despite his comic failures, his colorless public speeches, and his quiet manner, he remains a minor hero to many right wingers. As late as May 1965 while Mitchell, having been expelled from the International City Managers' Association, was trying to set up new chapters of the segregationist White Citizens Council, a member of Young Americans for Freedom referred to him as "that great American" in a letter to *The Buffalo Courier-Express.*

My own stay in the Hudson River community closely matched Mitchell's. Leaving a job as assistant news director for Fordham University—after having decided that informing the public of what it needs to know is a higher function than beating the drum for any one organization, regardless of how worthy it may be—I arrived in Newburgh little more than six months after Mitchell's appointment. Before I knew Newburgh was spelled with an *h,* I was reporting stories on the developing welfare controversy—the first wire story on the conflict was an Associated Press digest of a headlined article I had written after my third day in the community.

From then until my departure three years later, I reported the welfare story and the doings of Mitchell either for the Newburgh *Evening News* or as a stringer for *The New York Herald Tribune* and *The New York Post.* During that period I wrote background stories on the controversy for the AP and *The London Sunday Express.*

In getting material for my news stories and later, when I was doing research for this book, I had many cordial conversations with Mitchell, both at his office and in his home. I also talked to members of the Newburgh City Council, officials of private charities, city caseworkers, migrant workers, Newburgh Negroes, city religious leaders, and scores of welfare recipients.

I traveled to Albany to confer with state officials, to Washington, D.C. to interview top officials in the Department of Health, Education, and Welfare; to New York City to talk with leaders of Negro organizations, regional, state, and federal welfare officers, heads of private welfare associations, and deans and professors of schools of social service; and to Pennsylvania to talk to those who worked with Mitchell when he was township manager in Marple Township.

I am particularly indebted to Joseph G. Strack, Director of Public Relations for the New York State Department of Social Welfare, for his assistance in gathering welfare material; to Hilliard Gordon, managing editor of the Newburgh *Evening News,* for his hiring me to cover the City Manager, an action I think he often regretted; to City Manager Thomas L. Rose, for his friendship and cooperation; to those in Newburgh who would suffer the alienation of friends and neighbors if their names were mentioned here; and to A. N. Romm, editor of *The Middletown Record,* for allowing me use of material from that paper.

In editing this book it was decided to leave out many welfare statistics and surveys which, it was felt, would make the book less readable. I leave them for the experts and the authorities to state.

Statistics are necessary if we are to lessen the numbers and the hunger of the poor, on and off relief. But so is anger. And I haven't heard anger from welfare officials over the plight of the needy for a long time. This book is a plea for anger.

HAMBURG, NEW YORK   *Joseph P. Ritz*
March 1, 1966

THE DESPISED POOR
Newburgh's War on Welfare

ONE · A PLEASANT LITTLE CITY

MAY 1, 1961, dawned chilly in Newburgh, New York. Across the river the sun inched its way up the top of Mount Beacon until its rays began dispelling the mist rising from the valley below.

About nine in the morning a line of shabbily-dressed whites and Negroes began forming in front of the door to police headquarters in the city's gray-painted City Hall. The people in it moved slowly through the door, but the line remained through most of the day as others trudged up the incline from the crowded waterfront to join it. A reporter from the local newspaper described it in the next day's edition:

> At 2:15 P.M. yesterday there were approximately 60 persons standing in a Y-shaped line at police headquarters waiting for their [welfare] checks.
>
> They were interrogated in a small, drab back room which ordinarily serves as a communications center and fingerprinting room.
>
> Each applicant was asked to produce proper identification. They were questioned about their marital status, the number of their dependents, their address, and when they last worked.

The majority of applicants were women. . . . Quite a few carried infants in their arms.

A short, white-haired woman said she had been waiting for one and one-half hours. She was 71-years-old.

When [City Manager] Mitchell was informed of this, he immediately rushed her into the interrogation room. . . .

During the questioning, a woman [obviously not on welfare] came in and congratulated Mr. Mitchell for his actions.

"I think what you're doing is wonderful," she told him. "As a taxpayer I resent—and have long resented—my tax money being used to support many people who are capable of earning their own living. . . ."

Most of the people waiting in line said they did not resent being called down to police headquarters for their checks.

Whether they really meant what they said or were afraid to say differently is open to conjecture.

A vigorous dissenter, however, was a women in her mid-30s, who was wearing slacks and a sweater.

"This is absolutely uncalled for," she stated. "I have seven children at home. One of them is dying of leukemia. I should be with him now, not here."

The scene marked the beginning of the Newburgh welfare battle between those who believe government has a duty to aid the needy and those who stress the doctrine of self-reliance. It created a national fuss far out of proportion to the city's size of 31,000 people.

Newburgh is an old city by American standards. Downtown, a weathered stone house where Washington wintered during the last stage of the Revolutionary War still overlooks the Hudson. Until mid-1961 it represented the city's chief, although minor, claim to fame. Five hundred other United States communities fall within Newburgh's population range of 25,000 to 50,000. Many have the same problem of unemployment, lack of industry, and a welfare burden as great or greater.

.The land on which Newburgh stands was seen by Henry Hudson in 1609 as he sailed up the river which bears his name. The city was founded exactly one hundred years later by a colony of fifty-three German Lutherans who hoped to duplicate the wine vineyards they left growing on the banks of the Rhine.

Although vineyards still grow in the area, it has never become widely known as a wine-producing region. Because of its location on the lordly Hudson, however, it prospered. In the early 1800's, when the river was New York's main artery, it was the third largest city in the state.

Before then, it achieved historical importance as George Washington's headquarters following the Yorktown victory. There, for nearly two years, he and his troops awaited the official end of the Revolutionary War. It is a past of which the natives are proud. Most of them are lifelong conservatives (Franklin Delano Roosevelt never won a majority of votes in Newburgh for either governor or President, although Hyde Park is only a short distance away) and they frequently compare the city's fight against state and federal regulations with the War of Independence.

In a sense, Newburgh is similar to many old European cities where the mind of the community is focused backward on an active and glorious past, for the city is a dying cell in a very healthy body. That body is the half-rural, half-wooded area just beyond the suburbs of New York City, occupying a crescent located from forty to seventy-five miles from Manhattan. Already major industries are moving their headquarters into this crescent.

Already the homes of employees are beginning to sprout near the estates of the executives who make the area their home.

Orange County, in which Newburgh is located, is expected to double its 183,000 population in the next fifteen years. But the city itself is the victim of the same conditions which are creating growth in the area surrounding it—the national impulse, made possible by the automobile and the septic tank, to move out of the crowded cities into the more picturesque countryside. There is little room left in Newburgh to build the ranch-style and split-level houses young families moving into the country desire. To quote a 1961 city welfare study released by Mitchell: "New homes are not built within the city, but outside our line. The old homes get older, more dilapidated, and eventually are occupied by low-income families."

Although many Newburgers grimly refuse to accept it, as in many American cities, the older sections are decaying. Many of the brick and stone mansions and the wooden gingerbread houses on Grand Street, overlooking the river, have been subdivided until now four and five families live in them. In 1960, 17.3 per cent of the housing units in the city were classified as substandard and an additional 13.4 per cent as deteriorating.[1] Twenty per cent of its families had incomes under $3,000, the same percentage as in the United States as a whole. The median family income was $5,363, about $400 less than the United States average, and $1,000 less than the state average.

From kindergarten, where children are taught to read using a modern alphabet, to high school, where Chinese is among a wide range of courses, the city has one of the

[1] Comprehensive Development Plan, Towns of Newburgh and New Windsor, by Raymond & May Associates.

best educational systems in the state. Unfortunately, few of its graduates who leave for college return to the community. Slightly less than 5 per cent of its adult residents hold degrees. The median educational level obtained by those over twenty-five is a year behind the United States and state average.[2]

A number of industries have thrived and disappeared in Newburgh during its 250-year history. Once a major New York port, the last boats which regularly docked there were those of the Newburgh–Beacon ferry. The ferry line suspended operation in November 1963 after 220 years, with the opening of a bridge connecting the two cities. In the mid-1800's many whaling ships made Newburgh their home port. Its shipyards at one time employed thousands. But the last ship to be built in the city was during World War II.

Many of the textile mills and a major carpet factory, which traditionally had been a major source of employment, have either gone out of business or moved south since World War II. In 1956 a large manufacturer of overalls moved to another state. About one thousand jobs were lost. Four days before Christmas of 1962 a major textile mill, which had employed hundreds at its peak, closed permanently.

No major industries have been brought in to replace those which have disappeared in the last fifteen years. The only large industry remaining, a coated-fabric plant owned by Dupont, employs nearly one thousand. About four thousand other workers, mostly women, work in small factories or in lofts making handbags and women's apparel, but the de-

[2] The 1960 census gave 9.4 as the median number of school years completed by Newburgh adults, compared to 10.7 years for the state and 10.6 years for the United States as a whole.

mand for the products is seasonal and so work is not steady.

With the completion of the New York State Thruway in the late 1950's, and the opening of a segment of a federal interstate expressway connecting with it west of the city limits in the mid-1960's, the region's transportation hub has been transferred from the city to the surrounding area. The population center of the area is also moving westward, out of the city, a factor bound to influence business leaders planning to locate new stores and industries in the region. Each year during the 1960's, retail stores in Newburgh have lost business to suburban shopping centers.

The riverfront section of the city, once the main shopping center, is lined with empty stores whose windowfronts are boarded up or smashed. In former years ferries brought hundreds of residents from the opposite shore to the shopping area. However, with the growth of automobile travel it has become easier to drive to the new shopping plazas outside of Poughkeepsie, and the Newburgh stores have lost most of their eastern shore customers.

As the value of property in the waterfront section dropped, Negroes started moving there at a rate which alarmed the remaining merchants. In the ten-year period between 1950 and 1960 the Negro population in the city rose 151.4 per cent, a change which created apprehension and resentment among white residents.

This was the community Mitchell came to head in October 1960. Within a year the names of Newburgh and Mitchell would be on the front pages of newspapers across the nation, and neither the soft-spoken City Manager nor the proud little city on the Hudson would ever be quite the same.

OUT OF THE FUROR over the Newburgh welfare "revolt," the pudgy Mr. Mitchell emerged as the nation's most conspicuous city manager and one of its most controversial and puzzling political figures. Newburgh supporters praised him for his political courage in defying the federal and state powers. A few of them urged his election as governor. His detractors branded him as a self-seeker who, for his personal gain, waged a cruel warfare against those least able to defend themselves.

After an hour-long NBC "White Paper" documentary on the welfare controversy televised on January 28, 1961, he received telegrams and letters from throughout the country. Some strongly backed his stand with such statements as, "We admire your courage and agree with your principles." Others expressed the view of a Houston monsignor who wrote simply, "Shame." Even as Mitchell awaited trial on bribery and conspiracy charges a year later, he received hundreds of letters in which the writers expressed their continuing support.

The man who aroused such strong feelings is mild mannered, balding, and of medium height. Cordial, light blue eyes peer at a stranger from a rounded face, which is pale, even in midsummer. What is left of Mitchell's hair is sandy mixed with gray, like a field of dead weeds in the late fall after a frost. Although Mitchell was born and reared in the border state of Maryland, his public statements are read without a trace of a southern drawl. Only in rare, relaxed moments when he is conversing with acquaintances does a vestige of one slip out.

His father, a strongly religious man, was a teetotaler. Mitchell is a scotch-and-soda man. ("You can drink anything you want as long as it's scotch," he used to tell guests in his modest $22,000 split-level home, located in a new development near the outskirts of the city.)

Although a conservative dresser, the City Manager drove around the community in a salmon-colored Chrysler convertible or an ivory-colored Austin-Healey he retuned and refurbished himself. "I like hot cars, and I like two- or four-barrel carbs that'll let me go 150 miles an hour," he confided to a woman writer for a national Sunday newspaper supplement.

He considers himself mechanically minded, but admits he's a poor carpenter. His other interests are chess, at which he is a fair player, and room decorating (he insisted on having the ceiling of his remodeled City Hall office painted battleship gray to match the walls, despite the advice of lighting experts).

One thing both his friends and his foes agree on is, as a friend put it, "Mitchell is a hell of a likeable guy, when you first get to know him." Mitchell's appeal is not through any personal magnetism. The best description of his personality is amiable. In private conversation the former City Manager speaks quietly and is gentle in manner. He laughs often. Unlike some small-town politicians, he is a good listener who, in private conversation, reacts calmly when someone presents an argument against his policies.

But to those who are more than casually acquainted with Mitchell, he is an enigma whose personality and statements became more puzzling as the furor he created became more intense. In less than a year after his arrival in Newburgh many of the persons in City Hall who first thought his quiet manner indicated a measure of shyness which might make him too weak to deal with the city's strong-minded councilmen, were calling him "power-hungry," "domineering," "ruthless," and "politically ambitious."

Around City Hall employees knew him as a boss who became impatient if things weren't done immediately. He had a passion for keeping his desk uncluttered and the objects on it neatly arranged. He is a compulsive smoker, and has been known during press conferences to light a cigarette while a freshly-lit one was smoldering in his ash tray.

Mitchell's father, Rossel Edward Mitchell, was born in Tiffin, Ohio, the descendant of Northern Irish Methodists, some of whom had fought with George Washington. A self-educated architect, he migrated to the nation's capital where he married a Richmond, Virginia girl of Scottish ancestry.

Mrs. Mitchell today lives with one of her daughters in a white frame house in northwest Washington, D.C. "I'm 100 per cent for Joe," she told me proudly when I stopped to see her at her home. "I think he's fair and just. I know he'd never let a needy person go wanting." A serious-faced, gray-haired grandmother, her pride in her famous son is evident in the way she speaks of him. "I'm not surprised that he stood for what was right. He's always been that sort of boy."

She described young Joe as an easy-going, well-behaved youngster, who, in her words, "just took life as it came."

Both she and her husband, she said, were ardent church goers and their children were reared in the Methodist faith. "Joe," Mrs. Mitchell said in a quiet Virginia drawl, "was always active in the church and thrifty."

Of his religious training Mitchell has declared, "I was brought up in the Protestant ethic, although I'm not very religious. But I am certain that you are responsible for yourself under God. I feel that people are what they are because they want to be what they are. . . . I don't agree with the Freudian philosophy that man is helplessly guided by his subconscious—which philosophy is so solidly behind welfare thinking."

The Mitchells lived in a seven-bedroom, colonial frame house a block away from the Chevy Chase Country Club. Many of Joe's boyhood friends were the sons and daughters of prominent Washingtonians. But in the depression years from 1931 to 1937 there was little demand for the elder Mitchell's talents as an architect, and the family was forced to live on a very reduced budget.

Like many other parents in that unhappy period, Mrs. Mitchell confided that she and her husband tried never to worry their children about the family financial problems. Nevertheless, to Joe Mitchell, who was attending segregated grade and high schools during this low point in the Mitchell fortunes, it was a painful experience. "I thought I belonged in Chevy Chase," he once told me. "It was only an illusion. I didn't belong there. We were the poorest family in the neighborhood. These things eat into you when you're in high school. We should have been living in northeast Washington, but we looked down on people living there."

The first thing his parents did after they began to feel the effects of the depression, Mitchell recalls, was to discharge their Negro cook and maid. Although his father managed to land a job with the Federal Government in 1937 as a specifications writer, the family home was foreclosed in 1941.

By this time Joe Mitchell was married and having struggles of his own. He dropped out of high school in his senior year to elope with his childhood sweetheart, Dorothy Hayes, a slim, dark-haired girl with a warm personality. She was twenty at the time. He was eighteen.

Mrs. Mitchell, still a trim, attractive woman who speaks with a pleasant southern accent, said of her twenty-two years of marriage to Mitchell during the height of the welfare controversy in July 1961, "My life began when I married Joe. Looking back now, I wouldn't change a minute of it."

But Mitchell, the father of a bubbly teen-age daughter and a college-age son, admits the first ten years of his married life were "rough." After marrying, he worked at various jobs for short periods of time. He became a dispatcher for a fuel oil company, a Fuller Brush salesman, a construction worker, and, at the start of World War II, a messenger for the British Air Commission.

During the first years of their married life, the young couple lived with the rest of the Mitchells in a three-room apartment. "That was my father, mother, sister, and brother," he says. One brother had died. An older sister had married. Mitchell's mother was then working for the Methodist Home for the Aged and for the Georgetown Poor House—as a volunteer worker.

At one time during the early forties, four of the Mitchell family were employed by the Federal Government—Joe, his two sisters, and their father. Interestingly, his oldest sister, Mrs. Emily Lamborn, at the time of the welfare controversy was a division chief in the Department of

Health, Education, and Welfare's office of vocational rehabilitation.

"She's a liberal and a bureaucrat," Mitchell says of her.
"She disapproves of my methods, but not of my aims."
Nevertheless, there remains a warm relationship between
Mitchell and his sister.

"It's no secret that my brother and I disagree," she told
a newsman in a Washington interview. "But we're a close-
knit family just the same."

Mitchell still had not completed high school in 1944,
when, at the age of twenty-two he enlisted in the Army.
After completing basic training he was sent to Italy. On his
arrival he was promptly transferred to Dakar in French
West Africa where he spent the remaining months of the
war as a cryptographic clerk.

At the war's end in 1945 he returned to Washington and
obtained a desk job in the War Production Board office.
When it was disbanded, Mitchell secured a similar position
with the War Assets Administration. It too was liquidated
and Mitchell bounced to the National Security Agency
where for the next two years he was again a cryptographic
clerk.

In 1950 Mitchell transferred to the National Bureau of
Standards as an administrative assistant. He had obtained
his high school diploma by studying at night school after
leaving the service, and was now attending evening classes
once more—at George Washington University—for college
credit.

In 1951 Mitchell was called in from reserve duty as a
second lieutenant and sent to Germany with an intelligence
unit. He rose to first lieutenant before resigning his commission to become civilian comptroller of the 57th Ordi-

nance Group depot located in Kaiserslautern, Germany.

Overseas, Mitchell continued his pursuit of a college degree attending special courses offered by the University of Maryland. Finally in 1956, at the age of thirty-four, he received a bachelor's degree in military science from the University's European Theater Division in Heidelberg.

He returned to Maryland the same year and found a job as a minor official with HEW. It was ironic, and perhaps more than coincidental, that Mitchell should end his federal service in an agency with which he was to war so vigorously.

Mitchell relates that he was doing well in federal work, but he found it too restrictive. He wanted a chance to use his imagination and to influence people directly. His job as an administrator in the Division of Research Services of the National Institute of Health gave him little opportunity to fulfill those desires. Recalling his decision, Mitchell has said,

> I felt trapped. There wasn't enough human drama in a government desk job. I wanted to take part in the great sweep of human events. In government I could never see the results of what I'd do. I'd prepare a report or make a decision and that would be the end of it. It would vanish into a great bureaucratic hole.
>
> As city manager one comes in contact with the whole drama of human affairs. One gets a great feeling of reward. I've gotten greater satisfaction, despite disputes and set-backs, in the six years I've been city manager, than in my entire federal career.

At the suggestion of his father, Mitchell had already tried to break into the field of city administration. When still in Germany he became a cooperative member of the International City Managers' Association, an organization which was later to censure him for "unethical conduct" while performing his duties in Newburgh, and finally to rescind his membership.

From his overseas post Mitchell had applied to a dozen or so smaller communities who had announced they were looking for a city manager. None was interested.

Mitchell may have been discouraged by the rebuffs, but his new ambition to become a city manager remained strong. After going to work for HEW, he went back to night school—this time to do postgraduate work in municipal government at American University.

At the university Mitchell met Dean Seegar, Associate Director of the American Municipal Association, who had just been appointed Manager of Culver City, California, a Los Angeles suburb of some 33,000 persons, but one without its own welfare department. Mitchell invited Seegar to lunch and asked him if he needed an assistant. He did and Mitchell left his neatly arranged papers on his desk, gathered his wife and their two children, and headed toward California.

It was later said that because Mitchell was anxious to serve under the liberal Culver City administration he held liberal beliefs at the time. To that accusation, Mitchell has replied that he had no strong political beliefs then, although he leaned toward the Republican party. Some of Mitchell's papers on political theory, written while he was a graduate student, substantiate his right-wing leanings prior to his western trek. Nevertheless, Mitchell stated that in Culver City he felt he owed an allegiance to the Democratic majority who hired him for the $7,500-a-year job.

Seegar has declared that Mitchell found the transition from federal government work to municipal management difficult. "He was very largely conditioned to governmental attitudes," according to Seegar. "He would be working forever on records, on statistics. His office was filled with charts and graphs. But he never got out to meet people. Mitchell did an excellent job with our personnel system. But he made enemies by recommending a lot of dismissals. People were discharged who had been around for twenty or thirty years."

Both men agree that after four or five months at Culver City their warm relationship began to cool. "I had most of my difficulties with Mr. Mitchell over politics," Seegar says. "He was never one to duck a political fight."

Neither agrees on the cause of the difficulties, but it seems apparent that each backed a different faction on the City Council. Mitchell claims Seegar was disloyal to the Democratic majority which hired him to eliminate corrupt elements in the community. "Underhandedly he was working with the opposition," Mitchell says of the man who introduced him to municipal government work.

Seegar has hinted that Mitchell was interested in the outcome of the elections in Culver City because of political aspirations of his own. And he says, "There were some basic differences in our philosophies of government. It could be that my philosophy called for less management. Mitchell was interested in government that did a lot. He believed in direct governmental control in many areas."

Some news accounts have said that Mitchell was fired from his position by Seegar and the City Council after spending fifteen months in Culver City. Technically, the accounts are not true. He submitted his resignation on May 21, 1958, to be effective June 27 of that year, and was given a severance check for $1,000. But a Culver City official who worked with Mitchell said that funds for his position had earlier been omitted from the city budget in the fiscal year beginning July 1, 1958. "The elimination was called an economy move, but it was obvious to all concerned that there was something between Mitchell and Seegar," the official declared.

Mitchell's story is that when the Democratic majority on the City Council was overturned, "there was no question but that I was out."

His next plunge into community government was as manager of Marple Township, Pennsylvania, a wealthy residential area near Philadelphia. Once again Mitchell became a center of controversy—not an unusual situation for any city manager—and resigned under fire two and one-half years later.

William P. Davis, a member of the town board at the time, calls Mitchell's resignation "a matter of necessity." According to Davis, "He played one man against the middle. He wanted to create discord. I wanted to get rid of him three months after he came here."

There is much evidence that Mitchell's relationship with the Board of Supervisors was not a smooth one; there were, for instance, objections to press releases Mitchell was sending to nearby Philadelphia newspapers about community problems. But the answer about whether he was forced to resign depends largely on what township official one talks to.

Roy S. Benjamin, a second member of the three-member Board of Supervisors, says that the heavily Republican township let Mitchell go. "He resigned and we accepted it," he said. "He could have continued his job if he had wished to." In Benjamin's opinion Mitchell "did a fine job as a manager, but he was a poor bookkeeper. . . . It took six months to get the books straightened out after he left."

In Marple Township Mitchell's staunchest supporter is J. Frank Stirling, third member of the Board of Supervisors. Stirling calls him "one of the most efficient men I've ever had under me. I can only speak well of him. He was the most outstanding man of all we've had as city manager, head and shoulders above all the others." Joe, he says, resigned because of political pressure. "For the sake of his own career and his own future he just got out." Stirling blames the town bookkeeper for the tangled records.

Gerald S. Fuller, editor of *The County Leader* published in nearby Broomall, takes a more balanced view. "Joe was aggressive and personable," he says. "He was a better manager than a performer. Some men are like that. If he had been in a large community I don't think there would have been any problems. But in the areas where he had to do the task, the thing fell apart."

Only the men involved in the administration of township affairs can say definitely if Mitchell was forced out of office, and they do not agree. But there is one bit of evidence which makes one strongly suspect that his resignation was not entirely voluntary—Mitchell left Marple Township a full month before he could have known he would be appointed Newburgh City Manager. For the next thirty days he searched for a new position.

Comparatively speaking, Mitchell's plunge into the city manager profession at Culver City and Marple Township had caused hardly a ripple. Now he was about to kick up huge rollers to splash upon the national consciousness.

THREE · A RARE OPPORTUNITY

¥¥¥¥¥¥¥¥¥¥¥¥¥¥¥¥¥¥¥¥¥¥¥¥¥¥¥¥¥¥¥¥¥¥¥¥¥¥

IN MID-OCTOBER 1960 the entire membership of the New-burgh, New York, City Council met for lunch in the Green Room of the Hotel Newburgh. The subject of their luncheon conversation: Who would be the community's new city manager?

The post had been vacant since August 1 when the resig-nation of City Manager Albert J. Abrams had taken effect. In the meantime more than fifty replies had been received to an advertisement in the bulletin of the International City Managers' Association asking for qualified applicants to fill the vacancy. The list was weighted with some formidable as-pirants, including a United States Army general and a man holding a doctorate in city management.

From the time Abrams had first announced his intention to resign to become a top lieutenant for the state senate majority leader, the council members had been split over whether a local businessman or an out-of-town professional city manager should be hired.

In theory, the person selected as city manager would run the municipal government on a non-partisan basis for the councilmen, all of whom had full-time jobs. A city man-ager's position is similar to that of a corporation president appointed by a board of directors to head the company. Like a corporation president he can be removed from office any time by a majority of the board. Two types of city managers can work successfully under such conditions: a strong one who can impose his will on the council through persuasiveness and force of character; or a weak one who will bow to the strongest force on the council.

Pushing for the hiring of a professional was Councilman George F. McKneally, a grim, humorless, hard-driving plumbing contractor. "I was the one public administrator instrumental in bringing Joe Mitchell here," McKneally was to boast later. "It was the best thing I ever did for Newburgh." That claim soon was heatedly disputed by many local citizens.

McKneally has a Messianic attitude toward the city in which he was born in 1910. Like many small-town, middle-aged men and women who have watched their community change as industry moves in or out, as superhighways shift the paths of commerce, and as new nationalities and races move into the homes of childhood friends, he would like the return of the city of his boyhood. He would reopen the once fashionable stores along the waterfront. He would halt the flight of business and industry from the city and cut short the loss of the middle class to the suburbs. Foremost, he would stem the influx of jobless southern Negroes to the community.

Until 1960 McKneally's answer for solving urban blight through curtailment of welfare funds had gone untried in the city. But when Abrams resigned, the determined Councilman was ready to look for a man who would carry out his "solution." His solution made sense to many of the natives who heard it. Broken down to its simplest terms, it voiced their prejudices: The people who live in the slums create them; the slum dwellers are Negroes; therefore, keep the Negroes from moving into the city.

In 1958 McKneally publicly blamed migrants for the rise in crime rates, fires, and welfare costs. He persuaded the council that the problem called for talks with the city's Negro leaders, but nothing came of this. In 1959 during a session of the City Council he accused the city's Negro population of being Newburgh's biggest police, sanitation, and health problem. "We cannot put up with their behavior any longer," he said.

On September 16, 1959, in a speech before a group of Newburgh businessmen he said, "We must all work and demand a residence requirement in the welfare law. Outrageous as it may seem, people are locating in Newburgh without any means of support and demanding and receiving support from our welfare department."

"When you come right down to it," McKneally has described the welfare issue, "it's a Negro problem." However, to a point blank question he disclaims any prejudice. "I've done more for the Negro than any other councilman," he contends.

McKneally points out that he had been instrumental in hiring additional Negro caseworkers for the city's welfare program. He boasts of having gotten Negroes jobs in local businesses. He is proud of his brother, Martin, who as national commander of the American Legion in 1960 fought to end discrimination in its "40 & 8" branch.

He believes the Negro will have to raise himself in the community through his contributions to it, as the Irish and the Italians did. But he doesn't feel creating disturbances and using political pressure are proper means. Nevertheless, McKneally admits that the Negro, because of his color, has a harder problem in trying to attain a higher place in society. As to his public statements which have caused some persons to accuse him of an anti-Negro bias, he says he never meant them to apply to all Negroes.

In the community McKneally is known as a determined and stubborn man, hair-triggered to fight for his own way. In the late forties while serving as city plumbing inspector, he refused to participate in the prosecution of an accused plumbing code violator and walked out of the courtroom. Earlier in his career as plumbing inspector, he forced a showdown with the local newspaper when it editorially blamed him for existing sanitation deficiencies. Faced with a $25,000 suit brought by McKneally, the newspaper published a statement retracting its editorial.

Although he was just completing his first four-year term as councilman, McKneally was generally recognized as the driving force behind the council. While the other Councilmen took vacations of six weeks or more during the year, McKneally prided himself on never missing a council meeting. He was a frequent speaker before local service clubs and veterans' organizations. Like the other members of the council, he was willing to help a friend or voter through local red tape. He made himself available to the press.

During the welfare controversy he made a practice of arrogantly demanding national and international organizations to obey his wishes. Thus, when in the fall of 1961 Mitchell was suspended as a member of the International City Managers' Association, he sent the organization's executive board meeting in Miami a telegram demanding the City Manager's reinstatement. "This outrageous interference into local affairs will not be tolerated by this City Council," he warned.

Later, as a result of the unfavorable NBC documentary

on the controversy, he sent a telegram to network officials.

> I demand that the National Broadcasting Company grant
> this city one hour of free television time from 10 to 11 P.M.
> nationwide on a Sunday evening within 60 days to present
> to the nation the full and unbiased story of the welfare re-
> forms in this city.
>
> I also demand that you save all film taken in connection
> with NBC "White Paper No. 9" and permit the city ad-
> ministration to select from it such portions as it chooses to
> use in the hour so demanded together with such technical
> assistance from the NBC staff as may be necessary.

To McKneally's irritation, his demands went unheeded.

Former City Manager Abrams recalls that McKneally
would telephone at all hours of the day and night offering
suggestions and advice. Abrams, a highly capable and popular manager, was able to ignore most of the suggestions.
But Mitchell, who owed his job to McKneally, never achieved
that independence. Nor is there any evidence he desired to.
"For a city manager this [the Newburgh] City Council is the
best you ever get. That's because of one man, McKneally,"
Mitchell told me early in 1962. It was McKneally who later
broke the ties between them.

McKneally's sole supporter for an out-of-town professional
manager was Councilman Irving Green, a Republican like
McKneally. Green was a Brooklyn-born lawyer who transferred his practice to Newburgh in 1948 in order to enable
his wife to be near her ailing father.

The other two Republicans, William E. Doulin and William J. McIntyre, and Mayor William D. Ryan, the only
Democrat on the council, favored hiring a local man with
some business experience. It was natural they should want
to work with such a manager. They themselves were businessmen, born and reared in the city. Furthermore, in most

local communities "business experience" implies fiscal responsibility, enterprise, and a commitment to the power group and things-as-they-are.

Despite Ryan's being a Democrat, the four Irish-Americans on the council shared significantly similar backgrounds. All were products of parochial grade schools and were members of Catholic organizations like the Knights of Columbus and the Holy Name Society which demand devotion but no deep understanding of the layman's modern role in society. The families of the four had been in Newburgh for at least three generations and, with the exception of McIntyre's family, had been deeply involved in local politics. Ryan's father was a former state Democratic committeeman; the elder Doulin was once city Democratic chairman. (Ironically, his son in the fifties was GOP city chairman.)

Of all the councilmen, Doulin, a robust and jovial man with bushy white hair, is easily the most colorful. Boyhood friends remember Doulin as a skinny, scrawny kid who scavenged coal from the railroad tracks to bring home. "I've always liked to talk," Doulin once recounted to me. "Even when I was seventeen I was making speeches. When I was a kid working on the railroad I used to say, 'Someday I'll be boss of this town.' " Despite the lack of a high school education, Doulin's drive and quick wit, plus an ability to make friends made him a politically powerful figure and a successful undertaker, though not the boss of the town.

One of the banners in Doulin's 1953 campaign asked voters to "Put the Two Bills in City Hall." The other Bill referred to was McIntyre, a former city Democratic chairman, running with the blessing of both parties. In following campaigns he switched his allegiance solely to the GOP.

A short man with a round face and a ruddy complexion, McIntyre has a reputation for shrewdness and political savvy.

Like most experienced politicians, he knows the value of compromise and strategic surrender in order to remain an effective force in the community. Although known as a former Democratic official, from 1948 to 1950 he served as city manager under a Republican council. Upon resigning, he established his own real estate and insurance agency.

The fifth council member, Ryan, was a 45-year-old credit manager of a jewelry store serving his second term as the first Newburgh Democratic mayor in twenty-four years. (Under the city manager form of government adopted by the city in 1916, the mayor's only duties, outside of casting a vote in the council, are ceremonial—issuing proclamations, welcoming visiting dignitaries, and crowning beauty queens.)

After Mitchell's selection as Newburgh's chief adminis-trator, Ryan's voice was the only one on the council oppos-ing the welfare innovations attempted by the City Manager. There was a widely-held suspicion that as the lone Democrat his objections were in part politically inspired.

Doulin once remarked to me that if he had been in Ryan's position, "I would have had a three-ring circus." Ryan, how-ever, never showed skill for political infighting. Repeatedly in the welfare battle, Mitchell left himself wide open. Luckily for Mitchell, he had ample time to cover up while Ryan peered at his corner for instructions.

Although in the minority, McKneally continued to fight for a professional city manager. "I always put Mitchell first on any list of applicants," McKneally told me some time later. The plumber-politician admits being impressed by the glowing letters of recommendation Mitchell submitted. Among the writers were a professor of public administration at the University of Pennsylvania and civic officials with whom Mitchell had worked.

Nevertheless, it was not the recommendations which sold

McKneally on the affable Marylander. Like others who had met Mitchell, McKneally was impressed by his personality. "He brought me papers he could have well mailed," McKneally remembers. "He went all the way to Washington, D.C. to bring me a government paper on urban renewal. I liked his aggressive spirit. He had the energy to get things done."

On at least one of Mitchell's four visits, the Councilman drove his ambitious visitor around the slum district, part of which was to be torn down as part of an urban renewal project. "The ideas he expressed about urban renewal demonstrated he had knowledge," said McKneally. "Of course, his philosophy as a conservative was very important. I became convinced he was the man I wanted. Like myself, he didn't agree with federal control."

It was perhaps a strange statement from a city official who was asking for $2,500,000 in federal aid to renew the city. McKneally explained, "I differ from Mitchell in that he is a radical conservative while I am a reasonable conservative. Where the community has no other place to go for help, I'll go to the Federal Government. My city comes first." According to Mitchell's statements to me, however, he at the time was not as opposed to the Federal Government as he had indicated to McKneally.

Mitchell ended his job as Marple Township Manager in mid-September, while the Newburgh city fathers were still debating their choice for city manager. He went to Washington to stay for a few weeks with his mother and sister. "I was thinking of quitting the city manager business and returning to work for the Federal Government," he told me in February of 1961 as we talked of his past while sitting in his gray-painted office on the second floor of City Hall. But Mitchell was doing more than thinking about returning to work for Uncle Sam. "I was making plans to work for the International Cooperation Administration," he revealed.

"I weighed all that I had done in my life," the City Manager said thoughtfully. "I realized most of my experience was with the Federal Government. At that time my opinions weren't as strong as they are now. I said I would take another job as city manager for high pay and the proper environment." Newburgh's pay—$14,150—and its environment, apparently, were suitable for Mitchell.

Before the council met for its October luncheon the candidates had been narrowed to two—Mitchell and Richard D. Riley, 37-year-old assistant manager of Port Huron, Michigan. Riley, holder of a master's degree in public administration, had supervised the city's urban renewal project and helped revitalize Port Huron's sagging downtown shopping area.

As the councilmen ordered a round of drinks before lunch, Ryan's recollection is that he and McIntyre leaned toward Riley. The Mayor, nevertheless, still regarded Mitchell as highly qualified. Doulin stubbornly persisted in demanding that a local man be picked. McKneally, of course, wanted Mitchell, and Green sided with him. In such a situation it requires only a forceful man who has made up his mind to tip the scale in favor of his candidate. McKneally was such a man. Between the manhattans and the dessert Mitchell emerged as the unanimous choice.

Councilman Green told me a year and a half later that his mind hadn't been made up before the luncheon. "We were kicking it around and finally in the course of the discussion I came to the conclusion that Joe Mitchell would probably be the better choice," he said. Green said he met Mitchell only once or twice before the luncheon. Like Mc-

Kneally, he was impressed by Mitchell's voluntary visits to the city. "He seemed to be the type of person who would work on a problem immediately," the Councilman told me. And, in Green's opinion, Mitchell's personality was "a little bit better."

Evidently Mitchell was aware of Doulin's antagonism toward hiring a non-local man for city manager, for the big, robust Irishman was the only member of the council who had not met the candidate from Pennsylvania. Doulin said that at the time he was opposed to both candidates but that "everybody was talking about Mitchell, so I voted for him." The boasters, Doulin claims, included Mayor Ryan.

McIntyre, the former city manager, also said his mind was not made up before the fateful luncheon. "As we kicked the candidates around I gradually became convinced that Mitchell was the man we should have," he told me. As in the case of the other Republican councilmen, he didn't regret his choice until much later. "I think Mitchell has done as fine a job as any man could have done," he declared eighteen months later.

After the decision was made the council met in a public special session at 5:15 that afternoon; McIntyre read a resolution naming Mitchell Newburgh's City Manager. The council speedily passed the resolution by unanimous vote.

Reached by phone in Washington, D.C. that night by a local reporter, Mitchell stated, "This job is the fruition of a desire of many years. The combination of a beautiful city and a good structural government . . . presents a rare opportunity."

FOUR · THE GROUNDWORK IS PREPARED

A FEW MINUTES BEFORE 9 A.M. the following Monday, Mitchell, dressed in a conservative gray suit, walked beaming up the wooden steps to his office on the second floor of City Hall for the first time as city manager.

His first day was like that of any newly-appointed city official. He was interviewed by the press and had his picture taken signing a document at his desk. He met the heads of departments with whom he would be working and later looked for a house for his family still in Washington.

City employees, charmed by Mitchell's friendly manner, noticed only one thing unusual during his first week in office —the new City Manager was sending out press releases to New York City newspapers and to the national wire services.

Mitchell had been in office less than a month when, in November, Welfare Commissioner John J. O'Donnell, a 52-year-old city official who had worked his way up from caseworker to commissioner, nervously revealed at a council meeting that the 1961 welfare budget would be $983,085— an increase of $43,000 over the previous budget.

McKneally angrily proposed that an investigation of rising welfare costs be conducted. The proposal was granted unanimously by the council, although a study of the local

welfare department had been released only the previous
April by a committee appointed by City Manager Abrams.
The committee had reported that the care given to needy
residents was "superb," but recommended consolidation
with the County Welfare Department as a more economical
long-term measure:

> The larger area should provide a better and ultimately
> more economical administrative unit. . . .
> Arbitrary geographical boundaries seem inconsistent with
> present modes of transportation. We see no necessary bene-
> fit to be derived from a welfare unit limited to the present
> boundaries of the City of Newburgh. Duplications and over-
> lapping obligations can result ultimately only in additional
> expense to all.

Mitchell responded to McKneally's demands for a welfare
investigation by appointing three men to a study committee.
They were Frank Konysz, an unassuming accountant; Ray
Boyea, a gregarious movie theater manager; and Dr. Irving
Weiner, a general practitioner, highly-regarded locally for
community-mindedness.

Ostensibly, the committee was to make an independent,
objective study of city welfare operations and report its findings to Mitchell. What happened was something different.
Unknown to the public, meetings of the committee were
held in Mitchell's office with the City Manager acting as
secretary. Dr. Weiner, whose name was signed to the final
study report without his knowledge while he was on vacation, confided later that most of the statistics and figures
used in the report were procured through Mitchell's office.

Also sitting in on the meetings was Welfare Commissioner O'Donnell, a kindly but compliant man who might

have aborted the Newburgh program before it became a national issue had he been willing to publicly oppose it.

From December 5 through the end of February the committee held weekly sessions, starting at noon, in Mitchell's office. Usually lunch was sent up from a nearby hotel. Among the persons questioned during these meetings were Police Chief John E. Tierney, City Judge Charles J. Roskowski, and the Superintendent of Schools, Dr. Harold Monson.

During three early December meetings a representative from State Area Welfare Director Clifford Tallcott's office was present. But, according to Mr. Boyea, the men who came to Newburgh had an attitude so negative "that we just didn't invite them any more."

One of the representatives, Romain Brady, declared in a written report about a meeting on December 8 that Mitchell spoke of migrants being the city's main problem. The City Manager, according to Brady, talked of new Negroes replacing the old Negroes. The state representative said he "sensed the feeling that Mitchell believed there is a relationship between 'liberal' welfare policies and the influx of new Negroes."

Besides interviewing community leaders during the sessions, every member of the committee visited the home of a welfare recipient with a case worker at least once, and toured the Newburgh City Home and Infirmary for the Aged. While the committee was gathering material for its report, Mitchell was already telling local residents that many of their problems were caused by southern Negro migrants.

On January 8, in a speech over the local radio station, Mitchell told his audience Newburgh was faced with an immigration of families from the South "who have no visible means of support." He declared such an immigration com-

City Manager Joseph M. Mitchell (left) and Mayor William
Ryan discuss matters on the steps of Newburgh's City Hall.

pounded an already serious situation of overcrowding and inadequate housing facilities. Asked Mitchell,

> Where will these people work? What assurance have we that they will be productive to the community? Who sent them here? What possible good does this do for the community as a whole?
>
> Why should a city like Newburgh be the receiving point for a horde of citizens seeking a new way of life when we are literally bursting at the seams with crowded slums and already high caseloads? Is it sensible? Where does such a situation fit in with the general good of the city? Where will it lead?

A month after his radio speech Mitchell, faced with a growing deficit in his snow removal budget (the result of the most severe Northeastern winter of the generation), ordered the aid to dependent children and home relief budgets cut by a total of $78,660, and borderline cases closed. The City Manager told the public that the relief budget had been slashed because it was "the least likely to harm the common good among services rendered by the city through its expenditures." Ironically, a record number of 1,382 persons were on relief at the time. Many of them were unemployed victims of the same bitter weather which was forcing the city's chief administrator to hack off part of their relief funds.

The following day Mitchell commented that a city which is "soft" on welfare can expect to find an increase in slum areas. "Where the policy is tougher, you cut the incentives of the southern migratory worker to come in," he said. Mitchell's tough policy found equally tough opposition from the New York State Department of Social Welfare which declared it illegal. The City Manager, who was still unknown to the wire services and television networks, was not yet confident enough to battle the state. He recinded the order.

Nevertheless, Mitchell continued to be preoccupied with the welfare budget.[1] On February 24 a work-relief program was ordered under which able-bodied men and women would be required to work eight hours daily for their relief checks. The following day Welfare Commissioner O'Donnell obediently issued a Mitchell-written press release. In it the Commissioner lent his endorsement to unnamed future welfare programs proposed by the City Manager and the council. The release said,

> Some welfare recipients are under the mistaken impression that welfare is merely a program through which they can obtain money in the form of state and federal grants. I am convinced that there are many factors contributing to the problems of the city, which have been so eloquently revealed by the City Manager. It is my intention to prevent the exploitation of the welfare program by individuals in a manner which would make it contribute to further our existing blight.

The work-relief program was neither new, nor startling. Fifty work-relief projects had been in effect in the state the previous summer. City Manager Abrams had started such a program in 1959. It was abandoned by the time Mitchell ar-

[1] It would be an injustice to say that welfare was regarded by the city fathers solely as a scapegoat. The 1961 welfare budget was $983,085, almost a third of the city's total budget of $3,134,383. It is true that of the total, more than half, $559,275, was reimbursed by the state and federal governments. Nevertheless, that still left $423,810 to be paid by local taxpayers, a sizeable amount for a city the size of Newburgh. It was an amount equal to the fire and public works budgets and more than the $370,250 budgeted for police services.

rived, primarily because of difficulty in finding enough eligible men on relief to make it worthwhile. There was no reason to suspect the program, despite its merits, would not peter out in the same fashion when warm weather brought a customary drop in the number receiving welfare checks.

Until May 1 Mitchell's unsuccessful attempts to pare welfare costs merited little attention in the national press, even on a dull news day. He had forced a 10 per cent cut in the welfare, but it was quickly rescinded when the state Social Welfare Department protested. He had caused the closing of thirty welfare cases, but twenty-three of them were reopened, again at the prompting of the state. He had resurrected a work-relief program, but there was little chance it would have any noticeable effect on welfare costs.

But May 1 was the date of the welfare muster and afterward it would be a long time before Newburgh could again be just an obscure river town. The muster was an order by Mitchell to most of the adults on relief to pick up their checks at police headquarters. Its purpose, said Mitchell, was to verify that the recipients existed, lived in the city, and were qualified to receive aid. Critics of the City Manager's tactics were later to charge that in reality the muster was an attempt to harass the recipients and hold them up to public shame.

It caught the press, the public, the Mayor, and the City Council by surprise. The only ones who knew about the plan beforehand, besides himself, Mitchell declared the next day, were the Chief of Police, the Welfare Commissioner and the City Comptroller. It seems highly unlikely, however, that Mitchell would have taken such an audacious step, which was certain to be controversial, without consulting McKneally.

The reason for keeping his plan secret, Mitchell said, was

that its success depended on surprise. Just what was to be gained by surprise is not clear. The information requested had already been obtained by caseworkers in the department through visits to the homes of those on relief and was on file. Furthermore, the muster order didn't specify on what day the welfare checks had to be picked up. Those who needed time to invent answers to the questions of the police could have waited several days before appearing for the interview. In fact, a few recipients did not go to police headquarters until several days after the muster was announced, although there has been no suggestion they used the time to fabricate replies.

The letters telling the welfare recipients to obtain their checks from the police were mailed on April 29, a Saturday. Most of them were received on Monday, the day on which the checks were due to arrive. By midmorning the first welfare recipients had obediently appeared at police headquarters. In all, 250 of the needy were interrogated by police officers at the station. Eighty-six persons too ill or too old to travel were visited at their homes by policemen who handed them their checks after questioning. When it was over, the muster uncovered no unqualified recipients.

Reaction to Mitchell's move came within hours. "I might expect something like this happen behind the Iron Curtain, but not in America, and certainly not in the City of Newburgh," Mayor Ryan declared furiously. "This a fine thing to happen on Law Day and in Senior Citizens' Month." Reports of the welfare muster brought Clifford Tallcott, regional director of the state Department of Social Welfare, up to Newburgh from his office in New York City the following day. After meeting with Mitchell and Mayor Ryan, Tallcott issued a statement saying the muster was "not a flagrant violation of the law. But it is a borderline case, a highly irregular method and one which the New York State Department of Welfare could not and would not approve."

On May 17 a letter from Tallcott to Mitchell stating the city's action might jeopardize the state from receiving $150 million annually in federal welfare funds caught the attention of the Associated Press office in New York City. The story was sent over the wire and made the first page of the second section of *The New York Times*. It was the first mention of the muster by a newspaper outside of Orange County and, interestingly in this day of lightning communication, the story was seventeen days late.

But if Mitchell had any doubts about the support of his action from the GOP council majority, they were dispelled on May 3 when each of the four made public statements backing the muster. Most Newburghers strongly supported their City Manager. The local newspaper gave the muster its editorial blessing.

There was, however, a loosely organized local opposition beginning to make itself known. On May 4 the Newburgh Community Service Conference, representing most of the private charities and community service organizations in the area, officially expressed disapproval of the muster. It was joined in its opposition later in the month by the Newburgh Ministerial Association, composed of nearly all the Protestant and Jewish leaders in the community.

The clergymen's protest was mild, but it produced an unexpected reaction. At the second of the council's May sessions, representatives of the Ministerial Association presented to the city fathers a letter, moderate in tone, which protested the welfare muster as degrading. "We hope," the letter said in part, "any further investigation will not be dependent upon the muster procedure which includes the use

of the police station, but rather employs principles and tactics which uphold the dignity of man."

The drafters of the letter expected it would be filed away
and forgotten. They were stunned when the council majority
sternly informed them that members of the clergy had no
right to interfere in social issues and declared the letter out
of order. Commented McKneally, "If the Ministerial Association wants to do good, let its members go into the welfare
area and instill some morality into the people who are running up these costs."

Three weeks later the council rejected three additional letters written individually by Protestant ministers. Two protested the muster action. The other was in support., "These
opinions are outside the province of ministers," Councilman
McKneally announced. "They are out of order. I move these
letters be declared out of order."

According to most rules of politics, the councilmen's high-
handed refusal to accept even a letter from locally-respected
religious leaders should have been political suicide. But very
little in the Newburgh affair was played by the rules. The reaction by the majority of residents was to shrug off the incident as something prompted by a bunch of well-meaning
do-gooders.

In Rabbi Norman Kahan's words, the welfare controversy
"showed a complete lack of communication between the religious forces and the [Newburgh] public." There was no
lack of communication on Mitchell's part. "An intensive
public relations campaign has been waged via press and
radio, aimed at social reform, enlisting cooperation and support," he later told an out-of-town audience.

On May 23, when the Ministerial Association's protest
was made, the welfare study report, effectively sowing the

ground for all of Mitchell's future programs, was fresh in the minds of the majority of residents. Indeed, it was difficult for a resident to escape learning about it. It was printed in its entirety by the Newburgh *Evening News* in serial form after its release on May 8, and presented, bit by bit, by Mitchell in daily broadcasts over the local radio station, WGNY. The report consisted largely of a mass of findings, recommendations, conclusions and moral judgments, most of which were supported by little or no evidence, but which tended to support the unfavorable estimate of the public toward those on relief.

It said the committee "has heard evidence of the misuse of welfare funds, such as the purchase of whiskey, automobiles and other indulgences, with welfare money," but neither attributed the statement, nor specified what the "evidence" was.

It declared, falsely, that the majority of cases in City Court were welfare recipients and (also falsely) that migrant farm workers coming into the area tended to "affiliate with the welfare department as a matter of course."

It traced the city's problems to state and federal interference in the welfare program, the rising Negro population and a loss of taxpayers. It deplored an attitude of city caseworkers which favored helping the individual over the community, suggested that welfare contributed to the growth of slums and was a magnet attracting southern Negroes to the North.

If the ideas and terminology expressed reminded the reader of Mitchell's speeches, it was not surprising. Acting in his capacity as secretary of the group, the City Manager dictated all but a page and one-half of the report from notes he had taken during meetings of the body. In places, two of the committee members stated later, he added statements which had not been made during the session. (The page and one-half not written by Mitchell was inserted at the last moment by Dr. Weiner under the heading *Conclusions*. The doctor prescribed a state residency law and rigid enforcement of the sanitary and building codes as a partial cure.)

Despite its lack of depth and unscientific approach, the welfare study report was a surprisingly effective piece of propaganda. Not only did it plow and rake fertile ground for the acceptance of the welfare program, it offered a readily-quotable apology for the methods being used by the city administration when out-of-town reporters began asking for background material. In the early stages of the welfare controversy the majority of newsmen and magazine writers quoted it liberally without giving the reader the slightest indication that the report was somewhat less than objective.

When I wrote in a news story for the local newspaper that the report had been largely written by Mitchell, only one publication outside Orange County, *The New York Post,* reprinted the information the next day. Locally, the Newburgh *Evening News* buried the disclosure in the middle of a lengthy story headlined "Welfare Study Unit Reports."

Not everything in the report, of course, was false. Many of the statements were true and many of the findings were obviously valid, such as the one which stated solemnly, "The committee finds evidence of low moral values in the fostering of illegitimate children. . . ." But it also contained a great deal of hearsay and many statements which were false or misleading.

Among the things the committee said it found were:

1. A steady influx of outsiders [into Newburgh], principally from the southern states. [Ironically, the definition fit Mitchell although it was intended to be a euphemism for

Negroes.] These newcomers . . . are the underlying cause
in the steadily mounting welfare costs. They do not, as a
rule, apply for welfare immediately, but . . . their effect is
felt in the long run.

2. The greatest rise in cases has been in home relief and
aid to dependent children. [True.]

3. The high welfare costs and caseloads are related to an
ethnic shift in population. [Which is another way of saying,
"too many Negroes are moving into town."]

4. The accessibility to slum housing and welfare payments . . . [are] incentives for the influx of people from
out-of-state who will eventually contribute to high caseloads and costs.

5. [There is] an urgent need to have a toughening-up
policy on welfare. . . . The effect of this will be to discourage more potential welfare cases from coming into
this city.

6. The influx of out-of-state persons who eventually go
on welfare is of three general sources: migratory workers
and their families; relatives of migratory workers who
follow; [and] a possibly more than accidental movement
from South to North.

7. Social and economic conditions among many welfare
recipients are . . . worse than the conditions these people
attempted to escape from when they headed into the city.

8. [There is] evidence to indicate that New York State,
if not Newburgh itself, is known in Southern communities
as a haven for those who would emigrate. [Of what this
evidence consisted was never disclosed.] As a family emi-
grates from the South, it can get more money by going on
public welfare than it could by working in the South.
[Both statements contradicted the previous statement which
said economic conditions were worse than those from which
the migrants attempted to escape.]

9. The inability of the Planned Parenthood unit to advise

unwed mothers as to prophylactic practices is a factor in
illegitimacy, but . . . promiscuity cannot be condoned
and . . . the answer lies elsewhere.

10. The constantly rising welfare costs are related to
blight, and . . . as the blight spreads, welfare costs will
rise. Although the welfare department cannot of itself stop
this blight, it could be constructively used towards this end
by toughening-up, if local control were possible.

11. A majority of City Court cases are welfare cases.
[In reality not more than one in a hundred defendants were
welfare repicients. Yet the statement was published without
any comment by the local newspaper.]

12. [There is] no hope for the migrant groups in . . .
constructive community life until the population is stabilized
and the community is able to stabilize its social situation . . .

13. The broadening of the base of public welfare has not
curtailed social problems—it has increased them. Welfare
is now a magnet for those who would migrate.

The report suggested there was widespread immorality
among city welfare recipients. "There exists a high degree of
premarital pregnancies in the 12–15 age group in the urban
renewal area due to the behavior of parents, which is again
a reflection of the moral values of the group in question," it
said at one point. At another it declared, "The committee
finds evidence that the statutory rape laws are not being enforced in the urban renewal area, due to the moral values of
those involved."

And, in a section entitled *Moral Values,* it contended:

1. The number of persons receiving public assistance is
but a small portion of those who could qualify if they chose
to apply.

2. There are . . . many people who actually need pub-

lic assistance and are worthy cases. But . . . there are others who could and should avoid using public assistance in lieu of self-sufficiency.

3. The committee finds moral values in the urban renewal area to be creating a potential problem due to impressionability of youth. . . .

At the time Mitchell distributed the report to the press he declared it the best of its type he had ever seen. In view of his role in preparing it, his praise was understandable.

Even before the study was released, one recommendation had been carried out—the muster. In the coming weeks other recommendations would be incorporated in the city's controversial thirteen-point program.

FOR SOME YEARS before the welfare battle there had been talk of transferring the city's welfare functions to county control. It was a sensible proposal and a necessary one in view of the movement of industries and upper- and middle-class taxpayers to the suburbs. Newburgh, in fact, was one of only six upstate New York cities and one of the few in the nation which were still administering their own welfare departments.[1]

During Abrams' administration such a proposal had been brought before the City Council but failed to pass. Now the city fathers, faced with a growing tax burden, were having second thoughts. At a closed door meeting in mid-May Mitchell advised against consolidation of the Newburgh and Orange County welfare districts on the grounds that the city would have no control over who was to receive aid. He was overruled by the council, which unanimously voted for consolidation at the May 22 meeting.

During the session, Commissioner O'Donnell again predicted a welfare deficit for the year, this time one of $60,000. Mitchell added to the bad news with a statement that a

[1] The other five were: Binghamton, Auburn, Jamestown, Poughkeepsie, and Oswego. The Department of Health, Education, and Welfare had no knowledge of any city of Newburgh's size outside the state with its own welfare department.

$2.00 property tax increase would be necessary within two years to pay for rising welfare costs. It was a gloomy meeting.

The County Board of Supervisors' reaction toward the city's request to merge its welfare district with the county's was to refer the matter to a committee for study.

On June 1 Newburgh's work-relief program was canceled in accordance with a state directive interpreting new federal regulations as forbidding such programs. One man was on work relief at the time. This did not stop Mitchell from claiming that the directive would cost the city an equivalent of $2,000 monthly. According to his figures, the city had been using an average of more than one thousand hours of labor every month under the work-relief program.

At the regular council meeting on June 12 Mitchell told the administrators that a $6.00 tax increase for 1962 was unavoidable because of welfare costs.[2] In only three weeks the predicted tax increase of $2.00 had tripled.

The statement received little play in the press, however, because an action which was to have serious consequences was taken during the evening by the council majority. By a vote of 4 to 1 (Mayor Ryan cast the dissenting vote) the local legislative body voted to give the City Manager complete control over the City Welfare Department "even if it means losing state and federal aid."

The amount the city stood to lose was more than half its

[2] Figures presented by the New York State Department of Social Welfare belied the statement. During 1960 the city's share of total welfare costs was only $1,000 more than in 1959—$338,363 versus $337,329. Public assistance costs in Newburgh rose by only 2.33 per cent from 1955 through 1960.

In mid-1961 when the state presented its figures, it pointed out that Newburgh's share of welfare costs for that year "probably will not exceed the 1959 and 1960 shares because new federal legislation provides increased federal funds and lower state and local costs."

$983,085 budget—$599,275. It was a dramatic act and might very well have been a courageous one in defense of a principle had those who proposed it been the ones who would suffer hardship as a consequence.

The picture of a small community cutting itself off from the apron strings of the powerful federal and state governments brought expressions of admiration from the press and some municipal officials in other upstate cities. But the statements of commendation were mixed with words of concern after state and federal welfare officials pointed out that if Newburgh went ahead with its plans for local welfare control it could jeopardize New York's entire federal aid grant of $150,000,000 annually.

Joseph O'Connor, regional director for the United States Department of Health, Education, and Welfare, declared that federal aid for welfare is given to states with the understanding that all welfare operations within those states conform with federal laws. If there were any defection in any part of the state, he said, the entire federal allotment could be cut off.

While Mr. O'Connor's warning may have created second thoughts about the Newburgh welfare program in the minds of some state officials, many others agreed with Senate Majority Leader Walter J. Mahoney who said the state should encourage, not fight Newburgh's efforts to cut relief. A statement by then Republican Representative Katherine St. George,[3] whose 28th Congressional district included Newburgh, probably best summed up public reaction to the threat. "They wouldn't dare," she told the press.

In a paper written by Mitchell when he was doing post-

[3] In one of the biggest upsets of the 1964 elections, Mrs. St. George was defeated by an unknown systems analyst, John G. Dow, who became the first Democrat to represent Newburgh since the Civil War.

graduate work in municipal government at the University of California, he declared, "The grants-in-aid programs, ostensibly designed to assist state and local government, is the latent tool for federal domination of state and local governments by the alteration of the present republic of the United States."

Now, to all public appearances, he was striving to blunt that tool by daring to act in a manner which might deprive his city and his state of federal assistance. Some of the writers and cartoonists depicted Mitchell as a knight riding out, lance in hand, to slay the two-headed dragon of state and federal control. However, three days after the bold words in the council meeting Mitchell sent a confidential memo to its Republican members, which was never made public, in which he admitted that it was impossible to do without state and federal aid. More important, the note revealed that his much talked-about get-tough welfare program was a phony which he counted on to be squashed by the state.

The memo said:

> The corporation counsel and I have studied the law on welfare, and the comptroller and I have studied the budget on welfare.
>
> It is apparent, or indicated, that the laws on welfare would preclude too much local independence. It is a fact that, while we could go it alone for the last part of this year by paying our own costs in welfare, we could not make it next year without a tax increase, and that such tax increase would be less if we stay under the grant system.
>
> Lastly, to withdraw from the grant system this year would mean a 90 per cent cut in aid to dependent children allowance, and an almost complete lay-off in the welfare building staff.

Gathered around Mitchell in his office are members of Newburgh's City Council. Seated are George McKneally and Mitchell; standing are William McIntyre (left) and William Doulin (right). Absent from this meeting are the two other members of the Council: Irving Green and Mayor William Ryan. Green was unable to attend, but Ryan's absence was significant.

I must therefore conclude that while independence would solve our basic blight problem, it would probably rebound in political reaction and have the reverse effect we desire.

The public and the press, however, will expect some sort of action. I feel that action can be taken to our political advantage.

I proposed that the attached memorandum be sent to the commissioner [New York State Commissioner of Welfare Raymond Houston] and that he reply to it. His replies will undoubtedly be negative in each case. The questions and the reply would be made public, and would prove:

1. That we tried.
2. That we cannot act further.
3. The irrationality of welfare policy.

My consensus of the public reaction at this time is that it is at a high level of support. I believe that this type of approach will put an end to the matter, yet leave us in the position of having done as much as possible.

Your comments are needed on this as soon as convenient.

The memorandum to which Mitchell referred detailed a twenty-two-point welfare program as shown below. The points italicized are the ones approved by the majority of the City Council and are those which formed the thirteen-point program.

1. *All cash payments which can be converted into food, clothing and rent vouchers and the like without basic harm to the intent of the aid shall be issued in voucher form henceforth.*

2. *All able-bodied males on relief of any kind who are capable of working are to be assigned to the chief of building maintenance for work assignment on a 40-hour week.*

3. *All recipients physically capable of and available for private employment who are offered a job but refuse it,*

regardless of the type of employment involved, are to be cut off from relief.

4. All mothers capable of employment who are offered employment and who could utilize the facilities of day-care child centers, but refuse to do so, shall be cut off from relief.[4]

5. *All mothers of illegitimate children are to be advised that should they have any more children out of wedlock they shall be cut off from relief.*

6. *All applicants for relief who have left a job voluntarily, i.e., who have not been fired or laid-off, shall be refused relief.*

7. *The allotment for any one family unit shall not exceed the take-home pay of the lowest paid city employee with a family of comparable size.[5]*

8. The accounting section of the Department of Public Welfare shall be dissolved and all personnel and equipment transferred to the Office of the Comptroller, City Hall. This proposal is to reduce duplication in financial operations and to centralize financial operations.

9. *All files of all aid to dependent children cases are to be brought to the Office of the Corporation Counsel for review.*

10. *All applicants for relief who are new to the city must show evidence that their plans in coming to the city involved a concrete offer of employment which did not materialize, similar to that required for foreign immigrants. All such persons shall be limited to 60 days of relief. Those who*

[4] Point four may have been dropped when city officials learned that the Newburgh Day Nursery, the only one in the community for needy children, was licensed to handle only twenty-five boys and girls and had a waiting list. On the city welfare rolls at the time were more than five hundred youngsters.

[5] In mid-1961 when the thirteen points went into effect, the lowest paid city employee was a clerk-typist with a take-home pay of $45.09 weekly who was married, but without dependents.

cannot show such evidence shall be limited to two weeks of relief.

11. All persons on public assistance, irrespective of category, who have immediate blood relatives living in the city or its environs who are productively employed, shall be cut off from relief and the burden of this recipient shall be transferred to the blood relative.[6]

12. All prescriptions approved by the Health Unit of the Department of Public Welfare shall use the generic term for drugs rather than the trade name—this involves a considerable saving.

13. All medical assistance provided by the Department of Public Welfare shall be shorn of such luxuries as vitamins and other items not essential to the survival of those involved.

14. *Aid to persons other than the aged, blind and handicapped shall be limited to three months in any one year —this is a feature similar to the present policies on unemployment benefits.*

15. The names, addresses, relief category and amount paid of each recipient shall be made public by publication in the *Newburgh News* and posting on a bulletin board for the purpose of providing constructive help by citizens who are unaware of the plight of these people, and for the purpose of cross checking the validity of these cases through public knowledge.

16. *All recipients who are not disabled, blind, [non]-ambulatory or otherwise incapacitated shall report to the*

---

[6] This illustrates Mitchell's ignorance of existing state welfare laws—a charge his critics were to prove repeatedly. Section 101 of the New York State Social Welfare Law says: "The husband, wife, father, mother, grandmother, grandparent or child of a recipient of public assistance . . . shall, if of sufficient ability, be responsible for the support of such person." There are similar provisions in the welfare laws of other states.

Department of Public Welfare monthly for a conference regarding the status of their case.

17. All applicants for relief shall be photographed and a thumb print taken prior to the issuance of relief for the purpose of establishing positive identification. [Not made part of the thirteen-points, but adopted later in the year was the policy of photographing relief clients.]

18. In the case of families on relief, due to separation or divorce where the male member of the family is residing in the city, the relief shall be denied to the family on the basis that the male member of the family is morally responsible for the continuation of the support of the family.

19. All aged, blind, handicapped and otherwise disabled persons who have blood relatives in the city who are productively employed, shall be supported by those relatives and not by the city.[7]

20. All medical bills for all recipients with blood relatives productively employed in the city shall be paid by those blood relatives and not by the Department of Public Welfare.

21. *Once the budget for the fiscal year is approved by [the] Council, it shall not be exceeded by the Welfare Department.* [The clause, "unless approved by the Council by supplemental appropriation," was added when the list of regulations was shortened to thirteen.] This means that the Department shall take such steps as are necessary to stay within the budget, no matter what the effect on the welfare program.

22. *There shall be a monthly expenditure limit on all categories of welfare aid. This monthly expenditure limit shall be established by the Department of Public Welfare at the time of presenting its budget, and shall take into account seasonal variations.*

[7] Mitchell apparently forgot he had already made this regulation in point eleven.

The regulations which are in italics make up twelve of the Newburgh thirteen-point welfare program. A thirteenth was added when the program was announced on June 20. This was as follows:

> Prior to certifying or continuing any more aid to dependent children cases, a determination shall be made as to the home environment. If the home environment is not satisfactory, the children in that home shall be placed in foster care in lieu of welfare aid to the family adults.

The thirteen-point code, when first published, seemed quite sensible to most people. Ten members of the New York City Department of Welfare sent an unsigned letter to Mitchell which said,

> We have never had such widespread agreement on your amended program and heartily endorse every item. . . . We wish to extend our best wishes and success for the continuance of your amended program. We wish we had a few courageous civil servants like yourself in New York City.

A writer from Palisade, New Jersey termed Mr. Mitchell's actions, "A ray of light in a world that is on the wrong tracks." And a New Rochelle, New York man wrote, "I wish to congratulate you on the 'guts' you have in correcting a situation that is gradually growing to such proportions that the tax load to take care of the chiselers is becoming unbearable."

Similar sentiments were expressed by 90 per cent of fifteen thousand writers who sent letters, postcards, telegrams and checks to Mitchell.[8] The City Manager judged correctly;

[8] Many wrote in response to an organized letter campaign by the John Birch Society, which publicly endorsed the program. The volume was so great during the summer that an additional secretary was hired to handle it.

there would be a popular response to his program, but the extent of it surprised and nearly overwhelmed him.

The morning after Mitchell made public his new welfare program *The New York Herald Tribune* plastered it across eight columns of its front page and the *New York Daily News* carried an editorial praising Newburgh's action. Newspapers all around the country carried Associated Press and United Press-International dispatches about the revolutionary program on their pages. *The Fort Lauderdale News* commented on the program a few days later, "regardless of whether the professional do-gooders and the bureaucrats in our welfare department like the deal or not, we think it is in the American tradition that all those who can do so work for their daily bread."

In New England, *The Hartford Times* declared of the thirteen points, "Most of these regulations appear to make sense and will be generally applauded by the citizens of Newburgh and elsewhere."

The respected *Wall Street Journal* solemnly voiced its feelings on the matter with an editorial which said, in part,

> Unfortunately, not many localities are willing to give up government handouts, even though reducing welfare-fraud could cut off fuel for corrupt political machines and even help arrest urban "blight." But at least Newburgh has shown one way a community can meet its obligation to those who need help without obliging those who abuse help.

In Newburgh *The Evening News* guardedly supported the program as "a logical course."

Of the seven New York City newspapers, only the liberal *New York Post* and the influential *New York Times* opposed the Newburgh plan. Said the *Times,*

> The state has a duty to help in Newburgh as well as forbid

cruel and unusual punishment for the crime of being poor. Newburgh, enjoying know-nothing applause from near and far for "getting tough" on the needy, must be made by the state to realize that it is not a law unto itself. We suppose a great many cities would like to order their masses of poor out of town by sundown, or week's end. But what if everybody did that?

The afternoon *New York World-Telegram and Sun* declared in support of the Newburgh plan, "Too long have taxpayers shelled out money for the relief racket in this city and state. It is high time that welfare workers be curbed in their spending spree."

But it was *The San Francisco Examiner* on the opposite shore which best summarized the opinion of most of the public (including editors) on the issue. In ending its editorial, the Hearst sheet stated, "The idea of loafing on relief becoming a way of life is repugnant. It is expensive. The Newburgh answer has appeal."

My experience as a newspaper man has been that editors often share the beliefs and prejudices of the majority in the community. In the Newburgh controversy, however, the widespread editorial prejudice against those on welfare which pictured the average recipient as a dirty, lazy, able-bodied freeloader was at least partly the fault of welfare officials and workers. In their effort to protect welfare recipients from ridicule and embarrassment, those in the field of welfare have only made higher the wall which hides the poor from the rest of society and cuts off human sympathy for the needy.

"Had we been mobilized and campaigning for the worth of our programs and the people they serve, Newburgh and its predecessors would have met greater resistance, done less damage," Harold N. Weiner, executive director of the National Public Relations Council of Health and Welfare Services, Inc., told a regional welfare conference which met at West Point in May 1962.

On the other hand, the failure of those in the social service profession to erect signposts to guide newsmen along the twisted roads of welfare land does not absolve the journalists from never starting on the journey. In these times of telephone and hand-out journalism, there is increasingly too little digging into the reasons for budget appropriations, checking of the "facts" in a news release, or assessing the "truth" of a political statement.

Thus, by using a partly-fabricated welfare study report, Mitchell was able to con experienced reporters from metropolitan newspapers with circulations in the hundreds of thousands, and the wire services with a readership of millions. Too often editors send a reporter to cover a welfare story only when adverse publicity crops up. Only a handful of newspapers in this country have a social welfare specialist on their staffs. Yet, a third or more of their communities' budgets may be earmarked for welfare.

But welfare is more than a budgetary concern. If, as we say, in a Christian society we have a duty to help our neighbor when he is in need, we must first know what his problems are. In a complicated and massive society where it is possible to be privileged and not to see the poor, where it is possible to be a member of the great middle class and to know no one from the lower class, where our charity is meted out vicariously through some impersonal agency, it is the responsibility of the communications media to point out the defects and failures in our communities in order that a start can be made to remedy them. Too often this responsibility has not been met until a demonstration occurs in a restaurant, a riot breaks out in the streets, or a Newburgh welfare battle is fought. Even then, what is most often reported is the visual flaws in our society, rather than their buried causes.

SIX · WHITE AND BLACK

OPINION IN NEWBURGH may have strongly supported the new welfare plan, but the city administration's backing was not unanimous. By the end of June battle lines were being drawn between the advocates and opponents of the policy.

Among the first to oppose it were officials of the private welfare agencies. Of these, the most outspoken was Daniel Boudreau, administrative assistant in the county division of the Family Service Department of Catholic Charities. Said Boudreau, a graduate of Boston College, "The impression the public is getting is that those on welfare will not work. This isn't true. The area has been labeled by the federal government to be one having substantial unemployment.[1] There just aren't enough jobs."

Federal government statistics bear out the contention of the Catholic Charities official. In 1960 a total of 1,131 members (8.4 per cent) of the Newburgh labor force were unemployed.

Boudreau also questioned Mitchell's proposal to drop

[1] The Newburgh area had been listed as "having substantial labor surplus" by the United States Department of Labor since 1958. In order to fit into the category an area must have at least 6 per cent of its available workers chronically unemployed.

mothers of illegitimate children from relief rolls if they had any more children out of wedlock. "No one is in favor of illegitimacy," he told a reporter, "but I don't go along with the theory that anyone has a baby for a couple of more bucks a month." (Under New York State regulations in 1961 the most a parent could receive monthly in welfare funds for food, clothing, and incidentals required by an infant was $21.85.)

There is no doubt that the Catholic Charities administrator had genuine concern for the persons who would be affected by the get-tough policy, but the objections by Boudreau and other private agency officials were prompted by financial reasons as well. If the regulations went into force, Boudreau predicted, Catholic Charities would be under heavy pressure to distribute additional financial aid to the needy. "Our budget is small," he said. "We may run into considerable difficulty."

His prediction was to come true. By the following fall his office was forced to more than double its financial assistance. Problems of the local Catholic Charities officials were increased when some Catholic backers of Mitchell, angered at the organization's opposition to the welfare code, attempted to persuade fellow Catholics not to contribute to the Charities' fund drive.

Murray Gunner, executive secretary of the Jewish Community Center, questioned by a reporter on the same day as Boudreau, echoed many of his thoughts. "I believe that the majority of the public has been given the incorrect impression that most of the people are on welfare by choice rather than by necessity," Gunner professed. "I believe that most of the recipients would rather be self-supporting, if they were able."

There were others who protested: welfare workers; local Democratic and Liberal Party officials; Rabbi Norman Kahan, and a few white Protestant ministers such as the Rev. F. Morgan Roberts, pastor of the Union Presbyterian Church, who warned early in the controversy, "We may be playing with a kind of fire which will have a wide-spread result far beyond the bounds of our community." The four local Roman Catholic pastors ignored the philosophical battle, although the community is more than 50 per cent Catholic. The effect of the silence by Newburgh's Catholic clergy was to leave the lay members of the Catholic Charities office to fight without any expressed support by their local religious leaders. Later, a young assistant pastor and an equally young Negro priest-teacher joined the ranks of the opponents. In New York City religious leaders of the diocesan Catholic Charities office spoke out strongly against the Newburgh program.

The Rt. Rev. Msgr. George H. Guilfoyle, general director of the Catholic Charities of the Archdiocese of New York, wrote in a letter to Mitchell and members of the City Council and sent also to *The New York Times*:

> It is not only a question of legality. At the heart of the matter are policies . . . to which we cannot subscribe. My profound concern is with community attitudes and social philosophy which endanger suspicion and distrust against men, women and children in need. The remedy for these must not and cannot be left to the courts. It must be found in the conscience and heart of each of us.
>
> Catholic social doctrine emphasizes the obligation of society and its more favored members not to remain indifferent to the plight of those who suffer from poverty, misery and hunger. It is not a new concept in Judeo-Christian mo-

rality that there is a real obligation on the part of the community to provide decent assistance, consonant with the dignity of the human person, to those who find themselves in want or need.

One of Msgr. Guilfoyle's assistants, the Rt. Rev. Msgr. James T. McDonnell, traveled from White Plains to talk with the City Manager. Msgr. McDonnell, an outspoken, forceful priest, talked to Mr. Mitchell for more than an hour, urging that his welfare program be tempered and that a committee of citizens representing civic and private organizations be formed to attempt to solve some of the problems. "I presented all the arguments I could against the program," he recalled later. "I wanted to make our position clear, but I never heard from him again."

A few labor leaders, such as Irving Astrow, president of the Newburgh Central Labor Union, attacked the welfare code. (Astrow at one time acidly compared Mitchell with the villain of *Les Miserables,* Detective Javert, who dedicated his life to tracking down a man who stole a loaf of bread.) Yet, for the most part, union members and businessmen alike applauded the city administration on its action. When television crews from all three national networks arrived in Newburgh to film spot news stories and documentaries, one of their most difficult tasks was to find local white opponents of the plan who were willing to be televised.

Threat of physical violence played little part in the unwillingness of most community leaders to comment on Mitchell's tactics. To be sure, there were scattered threats of violence. Shortly after the Ministerial Association's letter was rejected by the City Council, Rabbi Kahan, then president of the body and from the beginning one of Mitchell's most outspoken critics, began receiving telephone

calls from persons who threatened to harm him and burn
his temple. And, at a Newburgh public grade school a
teacher asked if any of her pupils were in the rabbi's congregation. When some of them raised their hands, she told
the youngsters, "Your rabbi is wrong. He is sponsoring
criminal women."

Before the welfare controversy was a year old, other
critics of the program were threatened and maligned. A
tiny, bold-spirited medical caseworker, Miss Ann Power,
who frequently and strongly expressed her opposition to
the welfare program in letters to the editor and to newsmen, began receiving early morning telephone threats as
the conflict reached its height in midsummer. On two
occasions, Miss Power was frightened enough to ask for
police help. Nevertheless, she gamely continued to resist
the city's relief policies. When Newburgh officials asked
the state Civil Service Commission to eliminate her job, she
fought back by lining up state and former city officials on
her side.

A caseworker associate of Miss Power received a post-
card warning her "to stop your talk about welfare." But
more frightening, she said, were the telephone calls she
received at all hours of the night. When she picked up the
phone, she told me, she heard only heavy breathing, never
a voice.

However frightened those who received the calls may
have been, no one took them seriously enough to be scared
into silence. If there were only a handful of critics, it was
because the vast majority of the local population supported
the City Manager in his action and philosophy during the
first months of the controversy.

Said Rabbi Kahan, "People were afraid they would be
socially and economically ostracized if they spoke out

against the program. Initial reaction was definitely reminiscent of the McCarthy days."

Against such overwhelming popular opinion backed by the local newspaper and radio station and, to a great extent by the daily press elsewhere, those who saw possible harmful effects in what Mitchell was trying to do largely kept quiet. There was, they reasoned, nothing to be gained by alienating friends and neighbors or customers over something which didn't directly affect them. A local handbag manufacturer who spoke in opposition to the city's welfare reforms in a CBS documentary found business pressure so strong that he reversed his stand a few months later. (In view of all of Mitchell's popular support, it is ironic that the public castigated his political foes as vote-getters, while the City Manager was applauded for his political courage.)

In the Negro slums, created, according to Mitchell, largely by those on welfare, there was indifference about the subject in the early stages of the controversy. Early in July I walked down the main street of the ramshackle area asking those I met what they thought of Mitchell's program. Of thirty-four persons questioned, nineteen professed never to have heard of the proposed regulations. Eight were wholly in accord with the City Manager's aims.

I accosted two strongly-built men in their mid-thirties, as they were returning from the polluted Hudson with a catch of fish. They were out of work but not on the welfare roll. One summed up his attitude, with which the other nodded in silent agreement: "The city should get those people who don't need it off relief, so that some of us who need it can get it."

The reaction toward the city's new welfare rules among those I met that day differed sharply from that of officials of the National Association for the Advancement of Colored

People. In an emergency meeting of the Newburgh NAACP chapter on June 25 Gloster B. Currant, national director of NAACP branches, asserted that the program was the same as one adopted in Louisiana in 1960 "where 23,000 children were cut off and some of them starved." Speaking to some seventy-five Negroes gathered in a Negro Baptist Church, Currant asserted that Newburgh had brought to the state "the most objectionable Southern attitudes," an apparent reference to the hiring of Mitchell. The welfare report, Currant charged, had injected a racial issue into welfare reform by implying that the Negro newcomers to the city were persons of low moral value and without civic pride.

The meeting's only other speaker, Ellsworth V. Potter, Sr., president of the local NAACP chapter, contended that the city administration and not the Negro was responsible for the deterioration of the waterfront section:

> It is unfair to charge that the Negro is solely responsible for these conditions when the city administration has for years turned its back on this area. There are many contributing factors that have created conditions in the area specified by our City Manager. This is the oldest section of the city—250 years old. Its buildings have been neglected, its streets unpoliced and its housing codes unenforced.

The meeting culminated in the noisy passage of a resolution declaring the chapter in opposition to the new welfare program, since, it felt, it "discriminates against needy persons because of race." Telegrams were sent to the governor, the state's two United States senators, and to the Secretary of Health, Education, and Welfare asking for an investigation.

To the NAACP leaders it was obvious that Mitchell and

McKneally thought they had a weapon to stop the migration of Negroes into Newburgh. "The welfare program was partly intended to stop the migration of a parasitic element into the city,"[2] Mitchell declared in a speech taped for distribution by the conservative Human Events organization, one of his strongest backers.

In his standard prepared speech, given when he spoke to audiences outside Newburgh, Mitchell asserted, "We challenged the right of a welfare program to contribute to the rise of slums, to the rise of illegitimacy, to the rise of social disease among children and adults, . . . to emptying the city of responsible, taxpaying citizens and filling it with those who create crime and violence."

Mitchell and I discussed the meaning of these statements during several conversations in his City Hall office and in his home. "I mean that welfare is being used as a means of bringing the Negro up North," he told me. When I pointed

[2] The Newburgh "Report of the Committee to Study Welfare Operations" attributed the influx of Negroes to migratory workers and their families. Many newswriters on the Newburgh controversy have told their readers that the wave of Negroes arriving in Newburgh during the decade was caused by migratory workers making their homes in the community after arriving to pick apples in the rich orchards north of the city.

The evidence is that this is not so. Most of the Negro migrant workers are obtained from the orange-growing area around Tampa, Florida. They arrive in time for the apple picking season, which lasts from late August into October, and return South in time for the next orange harvest. The records of the local office of the state Labor Department show no worker hired through the office during recent years staying in the community past the apple season. Area orchard growers confirm the department finding.

From what can be learned, the first Negroes to come to Newburgh in large quantities were brought from Clinton, North Carolina in the early 1930's to work in the brickyards north of the city for a dollar a day. Most of the Negroes arriving in Newburgh since then were originally from that area.

out that 99 per cent of the arriving Negroes have no knowledge of the state's welfare laws, he replied that their leaders, the Rev. Martin Luther King, Roy Wilkins (executive secretary of the NAACP), and Robert C. Weaver (the first Negro member of the cabinet) were "mixed up in it."

Mitchell's attitude toward Negroes has been influenced by his border state upbringing. He is, for instance, an opponent of the 1954 Supreme Court decision outlawing segregation in public schools. "The decision was the action of a few people in power against the cultural mores of many," he told me. "It smacks of the reconstruction period and of the Civil War. It represents an imposition of the federal will upon the states."

Although he permitted his daughter to attend integrated Newburgh Free Academy (the city's only public high school), Mitchell fears that integration will result in intermarriage. "Then we'll have another bunch of leopards like you see walking on the streets," he expressed it.

Mitchell's boyhood was spent attending segregated schools. Race was never an issue then, he maintains. "We had the good old darkies who we called 'uncle.' There was no prejudice. It was a way of life and accepted as such. Nobody tried to yell about jobs or tried to move into a [white] neighborhood." He speaks fondly of the "Negro mammy" his family employed as a housekeeper when he was small. He is proud of having gotten a Negro a job—as an elevator operator—when he was employed by the Federal Government. In Newburgh he was instrumental in hiring additional Negro caseworkers in the welfare department. As these things indicate, Mitchell was no ranting, Negro-hating extremist when he was in Newburgh. His beliefs on the subject of racial matters were only as detectible to the public as his diluted southern accent.

It wasn't until the summer of 1964, after Mitchell had left Newburgh, that he showed unmistakably to the public which side of the civil rights controversy he was on. After months of being jobless, he revealed himself as field director in Virginia and Maryland for the segregationist (White) Citizens' Councils of America.[3]

If he could, Mitchell would restrict the movement of Negroes and other minority groups within the country.

"It's not simply a race question," he said to me once in early June 1961 when we were discussing the problem of slums. "It's a problem of low-class people, for lack of a better term. I mean it might be the Puerto Ricans or the Mexicans someplace else. What we should have are laws, similar to the immigration law, to prevent them from moving from one section of the country to the other unless they have a definite job where they're going. But, of course, you can't do that."

[3] Mitchell's efforts turned out to be hilariously inept. In late January 1965, six months after he founded it, Mitchell's "model Maryland chapter," the Prince Georges County Citizens Council voted to merge with the local chapter of the Congress of Racial Equality.

Tom Kelly and Clare Crawford, reporters for *The Washington Daily News,* who infiltrated the council along with more than a dozen civil rights workers, disclosed that among those given memberships was a Negro who submitted his application by mail.

The Mitchell-appointed council chairman, Norman Kilpatrick, was a worker in the Committee for Racial Justice Now in the United Church of Christ. The treasurer was an ex-president of a CORE chapter. Mrs. Crawford got herself elected recording secretary when she found she was having trouble taking notes secretly. Kelly was appointed head of the fund-raising drive.

At one meeting Mitchell lectured on what to do if a reporter ever came to a meeting. He also assured the members—only two of whom were properly segregationist—it was impossible for the group to be infiltrated by liberals. "I can spot a phony," he said.

Two weeks later, Mitchell announced his thirteen-point program. The eighth point stated:

All applicants for relief who are new to the city must show evidence that their plans in coming to the city involved a concrete offer of employment, *similar to that required of foreign immigrants.* All such persons shall be limited to two weeks of relief. Those who cannot show evidence shall be limited to one week of relief.

Later, when called on to defend this requirement during a debate with an opponent of his program, he declared:

Migration, improvement, and opportunity is the American way. But not at the expense of the taxpayer. . . . Someone wrote a famous speech about that once called "Acres of Diamonds"; your greatest opportunity lies in your own backyard. But anyway, migration and seeking opportunity is good, but that it reflects upon the receiving community is bad, and the people should plan, as we all do I'm sure, plan our lives, and plan carefully and have alternatives. We found that many of the folks that came into our city didn't. They just had no plans, they were just vegetables in a sense.

Again regarding the eighth point, Councilman Mc-Kneally proposed a harsher regulation: Send migrants (Mitchell defined a migrant as anyone not born in Newburgh) back to their place of origin if they have been on relief three months or more and have not lived in the city longer than five years.

The regulation and proposal were among the things which indicated to local Negro leaders that the get-tough welfare program was aimed at members of their race. "If Newburgh succeeds," said the Rev. William D. Burton, gray-haired Negro president of the Newburgh Ministers

Union, "then hundreds of other northern communities will adopt the same policy of containment that will say you can't move around freely seeking a better life and that is what we fear."

To understand the basis of the fear expressed by Mr. Burton, one must be aware of the modern phenomenon of mass Negro migration from South to North and some of the reasons behind it. Latest census figures show that in the decade between 1950 and 1960 a record number of 1,457,000 Negroes migrated from the South. More than half settled in three states: California, New York, and Illinois.

Chicago's Negro population rose from 492,265 to 812,637 in the same period. It is now a fourth of the city's total. Other urban centers in the North experienced similar great increases in Negro population since World War II. More than half the citizenry of Washington, D.C. is Negro. Philadelphia is one-quarter Negro. In 1950 Negroes represented 3.7 per cent of the population of Springfield, Massachusetts. In 1960 they represented 7.5 per cent.

As Charles Silberman notes in *Crisis in Black and White* (Random House, 1964), "Increasingly, Negroes are becoming residents of the Northern city rather than of the rural South. . . . Even at the height of European immigration to the United States, no ethnic group ever multiplied as rapidly, or made up as large a proportion of the big cities' population." By 1980 more than half the nation's Negroes are expected to be living outside the South, compared with 40 per cent in 1960 and 15 per cent in 1920. In twenty-five years predictions are that Negroes will be in the majority in seven of the ten biggest cities in the United States—Washington, Chicago, Detroit, Philadelphia, Baltimore, St. Louis, and Cleveland.

What Newburgh was experiencing was not different although in the decade before 1960, Negro population growth was greater there than in most northern cities of its size. The proportion of nonwhites in the city increased from 6 to nearly 17 per cent in the period, from two to five thousand. The 151.4 per cent Negro increase was accompanied by a loss of 13.6 per cent of the white population. The result was an increase in racial bitterness among the remaining whites as the colored residential area grew block by block. Once-proud Grand Street, at one time the home only of the rich, slowly changed into a street of rooming houses and multiple-family dwellings.

But the Negro population in Newburgh has grown much faster than its living quarters. Water Street, the main thoroughfare of the riverfront section in which the majority of the city's Negroes live, is lined with empty stores, their windows boarded up. Property assessments in the area have decreased more than two million dollars since 1950. Despite their increasing numbers, few Negroes have been able to obtain housing in the burgeoning new developments outside the city. In general, they remain restricted to the oldest portion of the city.

This is due not only to white resistance. Economics also plays a major role. Except for clergymen, an undertaker, and one lawyer, there were no Negro professional men in Newburgh in the early sixties, and the average take-home pay of the colored wage earner was approximately $45 weekly. With this sort of money—about average for the nonwhite wage earner in the United States—saving enough for a down payment on a house is impossible. The frequent result in Newburgh, as elsewhere, is families of nine or ten living in two or three vermin- and rodent-infested rooms. Some buildings do not have sanitary facilities.

Others are heated with individual coal stoves. Crime and disease, usually concomitant with overcrowding, are the highest in the city.

Yet the increase in Negro population continued without noticeable abatement during and after the uproar about the city's anti-Negro and antiwelfare policies. In an application to the Office of Economic Opportunity for funds for a Head-Start Project to expand the world of deprived pre-school youngsters, the Newburgh Board of Education estimated that the city's nonwhite population had risen to 19 per cent in 1965.

The explanation for the Negro's continuing to leave the South in spite of the miserable living conditions he finds in places like Newburgh lies in the changing economic conditions south of the Mason-Dixon line. In those states where cotton is still an important source of income, machinery is taking the place of the Negro tenant farmer and cotton picker. A generation ago four out of every ten Negro men who worked were employed as sharecroppers or laborers on southern farms. Now less than two in ten are engaged in agriculture.

New industries taking the place of cotton as the South's chief source of income have been reluctant to hire Negroes. For instance, although the number of persons employed in the textile industry in South Carolina grew from 48,000 in 1918 to 122,000 in 1960, the percentage of Negroes in the textile labor force fell from 9 per cent to 4.7 per cent during the same period. Rev. William Burton, who left Lumberton, North Carolina in 1957 to come North, cites a personal example:

Just as I was leaving Lumberton two new textile industries were in the process of being established there, both, I think, from the North, and an employment office had been opened which boldly invited "white only" to apply for the new jobs.

If the jobs offered were of the kind to require specialized skills or superior education, we might rationalize the priority given to whites and say that they were better qualified to fill them. But this was not true. The jobs, for the most part, required no education and only average intelligence.

It may be that the Civil Rights Act of 1964 will ultimately change this situation, but for the present, jobless and with little prospect of being able to support his family, the Negro is migrating north and then west in search of a future.

Mr. Burton puts it this way, "the city [Newburgh] should realize that when a person is hungry he migrates looking for food. He doesn't have to have a job offer. Any place is better than where he is. And there are tens of thousands of impoverished Negroes in the southern states."

The Baptist minister uses the term "hunger" as not only the desire for food.

A person can be starving spiritually, culturally and in many other ways. . . .

No doubt Newburgh has its share of welfare swindlers, just as has its share of thieves, alcoholics, numbers racketeers, dope peddlers and prostitutes. . . . But to use the welfare problem as a means of bringing reproach upon an entire ethnic group, the greater number of which by far is honorable and law-abiding, is a sin against that group and humanity.

Exploiting the welfare situation in an effort to halt the migration of Negroes cannot avail. Newburgh will get its share of undesirables as will other communities. It will also get a great number of useful citizens who will be an asset to the city.

The people who come here know nothing of the welfare system. They come looking for a job. Many of them move on looking for a job elsewhere. The people on relief wouldn't be there if they could find employment.

Another Negro religious leader, Father Elbert Harris, S.S.J., a member of the faculty of Epiphany Apostolic College, a Roman Catholic seminary in neighboring New Windsor, is also intensely concerned over what happened in Newburgh. As he told an audience of Catholic parents:

Any denial of rights to the Negro is a sin against justice and faith. Anyone can come to Newburgh, and nobody has a right to put him out unless he is a bad citizen, in which case the law will take over.

The Negro migrant has a right to pursue happiness and to earn a living, and no one has the right to refuse to help him become a more effective citizen.

The unfortunate story is that even when he arrives in the North, the chances that an unskilled Negro will be frustrated in his attempts to find work are very great. In the beginning of 1965 the Negro unemployment rate was more than twice that of whites. Negroes made up only 11 per cent of the work force, but constituted a quarter of the unemployed. In northern industrial centers one of every three Negroes was unemployed during part of each year the first half of this decade. A high proportion exhausted all of their unemployment benefits. More than 50 per cent of all unskilled Negro workers in the country were unemployed for substantial periods in 1963. And the unskilled Negro worker more than forty-five years old who loses his job has very little chance of ever again finding gainful employment.

The problem of finding employment for the northern

Negro is more acute because as a result of automation and other technological changes in the economy, unskilled and semi-skilled jobs—filled to a large degree by colored men and women—are disappearing at the rate of nearly two million yearly. Negroes also tend to be concentrated in part-time or seasonal work, and to be paid less for the same job than whites. The result is that even the employed Negro frequently is unable to support his family. One of every two Negro families live in poverty (although 80 per cent of the nation's poor families are white). In 1962 white full-time workers averaged $6,025 annually, Negro workers $3,799. To one of the nearly half million United States homeowners who has a private swimming pool, it may come as a shock to learn that in the beginning of this decade only two nonwhite families out of every five lived in adequate housing with hot and cold running water, a bath or shower, and a flush toilet. More than half of all Negro children subsist on relief checks at some time during their childhood, compared to 8 per cent of white children.

Four months before his death President Kennedy told the nation, "The Negro baby born in America today, regardless of the section of the nation in which he is born, has about one-half as much chance of becoming a professional man, twice as much chance of becoming unemployed, about one-seventh as much chance of earning $10,000 a year, a life expectancy which is seven years shorter. . . ." As Sargent Shriver told Negro leaders in December 1964, "The odds for that child have not changed materially. The odds for that child must change. If they do not soon, for many it will be too late."

Shortly before the welfare program went into effect on July 15, 1961, Rev. William Burton asserted, "If the welfare recipients had been white there never would have been a thirteen-point program. There would have been more consideration of the causes rather than the effects."

The minister's statement implied that the majority of the welfare recipients were Negro. It was a popular opinion and one still held by many Newburgh residents, as well as by many outsiders who have read of the community's welfare battle. Certainly they have cause to believe it. Many of the nation's magazines and newspapers reported it as a fact.

In reality, unlike some communities such as Chicago and Washington, D.C. where the welfare recipients are overwhelming Negro, in Newburgh Negroes have never comprised the majority of those on relief. At the time the thirteen points were made public, 39 per cent of those receiving city welfare checks were nonwhites. Admittedly, the percentage of Negroes on relief was slightly more than double their 16.6 per cent representation in the community. Nevertheless, the 359 Negro men, women, and children on the welfare rolls represented only 7 per cent of the Newburgh Negro population.

What misled reporters was the welfare study which used a graph to show that in 1960 a total of 337 Negroes received aid to dependent children, compared to 194 whites. It is the only category in which the recipients are classified as white or nonwhite. Interestingly, it is also the only category in which the number of Negroes outnumbered those of the whites.

Despite Mitchell's and McKneally's claims that the welfare burden was weighed with southern Negro migrants, in 1960 exactly $205 was spent on relief in Newburgh for newly-arrived migrants. And the city was reimbursed by the state for the entire amount. Mitchell's counter argument is that while the Negro newcomers may not go on relief the first couple of years they live in the city, a greater percentage than of whites go on relief eventually.

"Migration, improvement and opportunity," he says, "is the American way. But not at the expense of the taxpayer."

Yet assuming that the persons on relief are genuinely unable to support themselves (Mitchell's welfare crackdown uncovered not a single chiseler) and have no relatives able to aid them, whose responsibility are they? Had the city administration succeeded in shutting its relief doors to migrant Negroes the problem would not have been solved, only passed on to someone else.

All the hullabaloo about the thirteen points being directed at the Negroes was to most of the local public a spurious issue raised to cause trouble by the NAACP. After all, they reasoned, the new regulations applied to white and Negro alike. What they overlooked was that the harshest of the thirteen points, that which would have cut off all welfare aid after three months, applied only to three aid categories: aid to dependent children, temporary aid to dependent children, and home relief, which is made up in part by those working but not earning enough to support their families.

Of the 359 Negroes on relief when the new regulations were put into effect, 263 were receiving welfare payments under aid to dependent children or temporary aid to dependent children. Six of the seventeen individuals receiving home relief were Negro. The percentage of Negroes was lowest among those receiving old age assistance, aid to the disabled, and aid to the blind—the three categories excluded from the regulation limiting relief to three months yearly to any one family.

Mitchell denied the implication that the Newburgh program reflected racial bias. Aid to dependent children and home relief were singled out, he said, because it was in those categories that the greatest increase in the numbers receiving relief had occurred. And, he believed, it was in those categories that the greatest amount of "moral chiseling" was likely to occur. Mr. Mitchell defined moral chiseling as the obtaining of relief payments by persons who are legally qualified to receive them but can support themselves or their families if necessary—a contradiction in terms since under state law anyone who can support himself or his family is ineligible to obtain relief.

Negroes were merely worried about the long-range effects of Mitchell's policy, they feared the short range results of the welfare controversy. Their fears were not without cause. When Rev. F. Morgan Roberts talked about a fire being lighted which would have effects beyond the city, he was referring to the mass of hate material infecting the city from outside through wounds caused by the abrasion of racial tension.

An example of this type of publication was a four-page newspaper, *The Thunderbolt,* published in Birmingham, Alabama by the National States' Rights Party. Sent to Mr. Roberts and other area leaders, the banner headline in one issue proclaimed, "Impeach President Kennedy." Underneath was a picture of white and Negro children sitting happily together captioned: "Kennedy wants your child in this picture."

The bulk of the material consisted of a glossy-paper leaflet published in New York City under the title of *Truth Seeker.* "A journal for reasoners and racists," it termed itself, confidently unaware of any contradiction in the description. An article entitled, "Newburgh Rebels Against Bastard Breeding," suggested that the core of the national welfare problem is the bearing of illegitimate children by

Negro mothers.[4] The anonymous author predicted that whites in Newburgh were doomed to disappear, since the taxpayers (apparently referring only to non-Negro taxpayers) "will be forced to continue subsidizing illegitimacy, mostly Negro, and the number of colored dependent children by immigration will increase arithmetically and by subsidized local reproduction will multiply geometrically." Evidently the writer believed the offspring would be produced as a result of a love triangle.

A piece by a James Hervey Johnson maintained that

> The federal and state governments, now controlled by the Jew-led Negroes holding the balance of political power, will, by threats of withholding funds obtained by their superior means of raising money, prevent any local government unit from ceasing to subsidize the breeding of black bastards.

> The Negro and the Mongol surpass the Caucasian in fertility, which, under Christianity and Communism, the Jewish twins, is now the supreme virtue and the means of conquest.

Fifteen hundred copies of this egregious nonsense were mailed to leading citizens in the community, including city officials and the newspaper, with the injunction that they

---

[4] Nearly a fourth of all Negro babies are illegitimate. Only about 20 per cent of all illegitimate children, black or white, however, are beneficiaries of the federal-state relief grant programs in operation in the fifty states. There is no reason to believe that cutting off aid to illegitimate children would decrease the numbers of babies being born out of wedlock, since most of them are the result of the satisfaction of an immediate desire. It might, should the taxpayer desire, decrease the population of illegitimate children through starvation and poor health.

Any girl who has a baby for the sake of the dollar a day that welfare pays is not only immoral but stupid. There are far easier ways for a woman to earn sin money.

"be read by public officials and other influential citizens in every community where welfare relief increases the percentage of colored people."

"Whether we like it or not," Rev. F. Morgan Roberts told his congregation, "there are some aspects of our Newburgh controversy which have evidently utterly delighted the Gestapo, Ku Klux Klan, and assorted hate groups which have a real organized existence in our society."

Whatever their own racial views were, neither Mitchell nor McKneally could stomach the messages of hate flooding the city through the gates they had inadvertently opened.

"It's hurting our cause badly," Mitchell admitted.

McKneally flatly stated, "The only thing I can do is express disgust with it."

One hundred copies of the *Truth Seeker* found in the possession of two city employees—members of the meter division of the police department—were confiscated and the men warned by the City Manager that if they were ever caught with the material again they would be discharged.

The treatment afforded the Arkansas-born editor of the racist pamphlet, Charles Smith, when he arrived in early August to distribute his literature was harsher. As he stood outside the county court house handing out his inflamatory throwaways to whites and Negroes alike, he was arrested and jailed on a disorderly conduct charge. After a trial before the city judge several days later, the then seventy-three-year-old editor was found guilty, fined $10 and sentenced to a ten day jail term. The conviction was reversed in county court a little more than a year later by Judge Edward M. O'Gorman who observed that anyone in this country, under ordinary circumstances, has the right to speak freely in behalf of his ideas.

It was not the last that would be heard of Smith or his publication in connection with Newburgh affairs.

The poisons seeping in from the outside during the summer of 1961 helped to increase racial tension, already taut. Fortunately, there was no violence. Ironically, the potentially most dangerous situation was created not by whites, but by outside Negro agitators. It arose when members of the anti-white Black Muslim cult scheduled a trip from New York City to Newburgh in order to demonstrate in front of Mitchell's City Hall office. Worried city fathers alerted the police force to station extra men in the City Hall area. They were not needed. Only three or four members of the cult were on hand to board the Newburgh-bound bus and the demonstration was canceled.

Since the emotionally torrid summer of 1961 racial tensions have slackened somewhat. There is little likelihood now of a small incident sparking off a riot between the races as was feared then. One beneficial happening growing out of the dangerous situation has been the formation by community-minded men and women of a Committee on Human Relations which has as one of its chief goals the easing of racial abrasions.

But relationships between whites and Negroes have not returned even to the uneasy level that existed before the welfare controversy. Despite all the evidence to the contrary, in the minds of many Newburghers the welfare problem is still largely the fault of the Negro. Resentment between the races bubbles to the surface in battles over such things as school district boundaries and the location of new public housing developments.

In the spring of 1965, white residents in a middle-class section of Newburgh expressed vehemence at the announcement by a new city administration that it would locate a low-income housing project in their midst. Believing that the project would be largely occupied by Negroes, they packed public hearings on rezoning the area. An example of the antagonism toward the Negro which Mitchell solidified occurred during one of the heated sessions when a member of the audience rose and exclaimed, "What we need is Mitchell back." The majority of the audience cheered.

Although also the product of a border state with a strong segregationist tradition, Mitchell's successor, Thomas L. Rose, a Kentuckian, was sympathic to the Negroes' problems and aspirations. Unlike many native Newburghers who recoiled at the thought of having a Negro neighbor, Rose demonstrated his amiability toward members of the race by moving his family into a mixed neighborhood shortly after coming to the city in 1964.

The changed mood at City Hall on the race issue is best illustrated by two events: the decision by the administration and a new council majority to move the site of the housing project from the Negro slum area—where it would have been a high-rise ghetto—to a white, middle-class neighborhood; and the hiring of a Negro accountant as city finance director in April 1965, the first member of his race to hold a high-level city office. Both events would have been unthinkable during Newburgh's stormy Mitchell-McKneally era.

The ultimate contrast occurred on March 1, 1966, when the Negro finance director became acting city manager in place of Rose who was on his way to Vietnam as a civilian advisor in local government.

In the Negro community a new militant, articulate leadership has taken over which is resolved to prevent any future local programs aimed against members of their race. Its head, a young Harvard-educated minister who came to Newburgh in 1964 because he thought the Negro community needed continual leadership, told me a year later, "The next time we will move to stop this before it gets too big."

The minister, the Rev. Frank Jones, pastor of Newburgh's AME Zion Church, and the new executive secretary of the city's branch of the NAACP, played a role in the selection of a Negro city finance director and was one of the founders of a Committee for Social Action set up to develop programs to alleviate the conditions of poverty and eliminate its causes.

Negro leaders like Frank Jones and William Burton are sensitive to the dangers in political programs, like Newburgh's, which can fan the fires of prejudice to smokescreen its own ineptness and unwillingness to deal with the basic causes of the community's problems. Snug in their status as members of the majority, most whites were blinded to any peril in the city's policies during the height of the welfare controversy in the summer of 1961.

An exception was a Newburgh lawyer who, in a letter to *The Evening News,* wrote of his distress over the injection of race into the battle. What the attorney, Seymour Greenblatt, said is worth repeating here:

Public assistance is not provided solely to one people or one race. The problem of public assistance and those that may be taking improper advantage of some of its provisions should be treated on an individual basis. A man in need should be judged upon his needs and not upon his ancestry or place of birth.

Liberty and equality are precious rights and an attack upon any minority group will . . . affect each one of us.

NATIONWIDE, initial reaction to the Newburgh welfare experiment was overwhelmingly favorable. The notion that persons have to be on relief has never been accepted by the majority of taxpayers. The city was lauded for ridding the taxpayer of the burden of supporting loafers and immorality, not only by the press and a few thousand letter writers, but also by the masses of working people and businessmen.

In a poll conducted among nearly three thousand readers of the *New York Daily Mirror,* Newburgh's welfare proposal drew the approval of nearly 95 per cent. A national Gallup poll reported on August 13, 1961, that 85 per cent of all Americans questioned approved key provisions of the plan.

A private poll conducted about the same time for Governor Nelson A. Rockefeller by the Political Analysis Associates of Princeton, New Jersey disclosed that approximately one-third of those interviewed believed 40 per cent or more of all welfare recipients are chiselers. Almost as many believed that between 11 and 39 per cent were chiseling.[1] Another Gallup poll revealed early in 1965 that only 43 per cent of those questioned had a favorable at-

[1] Moreland Commission Report "Public Welfare in the State of New York," January 15, 1963.

titude toward welfare and relief programs. The most frequently expressed criticism was the belief that a large number of persons get relief without deserving it.

In view of the overwhelming backing the Newburgh program received at the outset, it was not surprising that support for it was voiced in both houses of Congress. Representative William Jennings Bryan Dorn, Democrat of South Carolina, introduced a bill (never passed) to authorize local communities to control, in general, their own work-relief programs. "The City of Newburgh," Dorn told the House, "in formulating recent welfare and relief regulations acted properly and wisely in the best interest of her people."

On the other side of the House, Republican Steven B. Derounian of New York commented, "Newburgh, against many odds, is fighting a mounting social problem which is duplicated over and over across the nation." Republican Katharine St. George declared, "This is the first time since the Boston Tea Party that the citizens themselves have decided to take matters in their own hands, to correct abuses themselves and to run their own affair." In the Senate, Barry Goldwater told newsmen, "I'd like to see the [Newburgh] plan in every city in America."

For a time, it looked as though local and state legislatures and welfare officials throughout the country might adopt some part of the Newburgh plan. Official notice of support reached Mitchell from as far as the West Coast, where the Inter-City Council of Santa Clara County, California voted its backing.

Five citizens of Bartlesville, Oklahoma wrote asking for copies of the thirteen points so they could ask their state legislature to adopt them. Legislators in Utah, Arizona, New Jersey, and Georgia requested copies in order to introduce some of the points into their state welfare programs. Among others making the request was the director of the Office of Territories of the United States Department of Interior. "This problem of public assistance is of concern to our territorial Government," the federal official, Richard F. Taitano, wrote.

The program was exported to Latin America. Copies of the thirteen points were sent to the director of Catholic Relief Services for the National Catholic Welfare Conference in Asuncion, Paraguay at his request.

In Richmond, Virginia the City Manager, Horace E. Edwards, proposed to try the Newburgh plan there. The manager of the Town of Mansfield, Massachusetts expressed a similar intent. A candidate for the mayoralty of Springfield, Massachusetts flew in a private plane to Newburgh in order to converse with Mitchell about the thirteen points. And, a group of county supervisors from three northern California counties crossed the continent to meet with Mitchell and take home some of his thoughts on welfare reform.

Within the State of New York, the upstate city of Oneida announced a welfare crackdown which the welfare commissioner promised would "achieve as much or more than the Newburgh Welfare Department is attempting to do." The welfare commissioner of Oswego, another upstate city, asked for copies of the thirteen points and offered to testify "to the bad conditions which exist under the present welfare setup," if Mitchell needed his support.

The Jefferson County (New York) Board of Supervisors passed a resolution unanimously backing the Newburgh program. The State Supervisors Association, whose members gave Mitchell a standing ovation after he spoke before them, unanimously passed a resolution condemning "obsolete practices, principles and philosophies" in public welfare.

In early December 1961 a conference of state Hi-Y Youths passed, 85 to 5, a six-point welfare program based on the Newburgh measures.[2]

Earlier, Young Americans for Freedom, a national conservative youth organization which then claimed more than twenty-five thousand members, endorsed the program and praised the city for its "courageous stand in the welfare controversy."

It is doubtful if those who so strongly supported all of the thirteen points would have been so enthusiastic had they realized that the harshest—that limiting relief to three months—was directed primarily at children, instead of the large numbers of able-bodied they assumed remained after the aged, the disabled, and the blind were excluded. Oddly

[2] Among the Hi-Y delegates lobbying for the bill was Christopher Dunleavy, a nephew of Councilman George McKneally. The six-point resolution, however, was introduced by Charles Stenger of Olean and Lawrence Rice of Buffalo, a Negro delegate.

The six points, approved on December 10, 1961, were: 1. Relief payments other than to the aged, blind or disabled shall be limited to three months in any one year. 2. Able-bodied men shall be denied welfare if they refuse to take a legitimate job offer even if the offer is not in their usual line of work. 3. Men quitting jobs for no reason shall lose relief payments. 4. Men who receive social welfare and ADC (Aid to Dependent Children) who cannot otherwise find jobs shall be put to work by state, county, or city public works departments at the minimum wage. No person shall be required to work for more than the number of days necessary to earn such amount or to be paid more than the number of days totaling eight hours a day and 40 in a week. Any person who refused to report for or to perform work to which he has been assigned by the public welfare official shall thereupon become ineligible for home relief and ADC. 5. Unmarried mothers shall be denied relief if after being on welfare they have more children out of wedlock. 6. No family's allotment shall exceed the take home pay of the lowest paid city employee with a comparable-sized family in the location concerned.

enough, no one in the welfare field publicly pointed out this fact.

However, not all legislators, even in New York, were as enthusiastic about the welfare program as those quoted in the last few pages. New York State Assembly Speaker Joseph P. Carlino, for instance, said he sympathized with Newburgh's efforts to cut relief costs, but he didn't think the way to do it was by cutting persons off the relief rolls after three months, or deny aid to mothers who continue to bear illegitimate children. "I'm old fashioned enough to think that no one wants to go on relief, that people want a job and to raise their families decently. Only there are some parts of the country where the opportunities don't seem to be available."

There were other powerful state forces marshaled against Mitchell in early summer 1961. For one thing, his widespread support did not intimidate members of the New York State Board of Social Welfare, an independent body whose members are appointed by the governor but not controled by him or the state legislature. Said the board's chairman, Myles A. Amend, a New York City lawyer, "Some of the thirteen points are inhuman and indecent, most of them are illegal and the others are unnecessary."

On June 29, 1961, Mitchell and eight other city officials received subpoenas to appear before a committee of the board at a public hearing on the city's administration of welfare regulations. Among those subpoenaed were all five members of the City Council and Welfare Commissioner O'Donnell.

Mitchell boasted to the press he might defy the subpoena on the ground that the committee had no right to issue it. "We are not pawns of the state Board of Social Welfare," he argued. "Use of the subpoena for welfare purposes is nor-

"But I'm Just Trying to Clean Up the Mess!"

Courtesy of Rochester (N.Y.) *Times-Union*

mally confined to welfare recipients," he contended. "We are not convinced the board has the right to subpoena municipal officials."

The hearing was held in Albany on July 7. All those subpoenaed, including Mitchell, were present. The irrepressible City Manager distributed to the press copies of a more than five thousand-word prepared statement he intended to make to the board members.

The city, said Mitchell, had no intention of "depriving the truly needy of aid and comfort." He continued, "On the other hand, neither shall the city suffer, and neither shall the city as a whole be the subject, if we can avoid it, to further economic and social deterioration." The city manager's sometimes awkwardly-worded remarks not only added up to a rambling statement of defiance, they also suggested that the city intended to make its program more disagreeable to the state board. And it charged welfare with financing crime, illegitimacy, disease, and other social evils.

> I and the members of the City Council are in favor of the ideology of welfare as it pertains to the use of public funds to safeguard the life and security of the indigent, of the destitute, of the disabled, of the aged, of the handicapped, and of the socially maladjusted citizens.

But, continued the City Manager,

> our position is that unless welfare considers the perspective of the community's total economic and social situation, work on individual cases is futile and wasteful. No arm of the government, anywhere, has the right to spend tax dollars with no tangible results for the community as a whole. . . . We have spent in Newburgh over the past eleven years $8,800,000 of public funds (including state and federal funds) on various categories of welfare. During this

time our social and economic problems have not been reduced, they have been compounded.

Mitchell claimed that the various welfare programs then in operation represented a transference of the responsibilities of families to taxpayers. "This is not in full accord with our viewpoints of family responsibilities," he said.

There was a hint that aid to the disabled and to the aged might next be curtailed if Newburgh was successful in putting its program into effect. Said Mitchell, "We have taken no steps in the aged and disabled categories at this time in order to attack first the most telling categories."

He also made a direct threat to chop the payroll and personnel of the city welfare department. We have plans for administrative reorganization, he asserted, "for we feel that eventually some action must be taken to reduce an overhead cost of 17 per cent in [welfare] administration."

He maintained that the city's greatest problem was aid to dependent children:

By its very definition it is an aid category involving a broken home. It involves illegitimacy, separations, divorces, widows, but largely it is the mirror of the sordid part of society. Its rise indicates a failure of the welfare program in its responsibility to the community as a whole.

The City Manager rejected the charge that his program was directed at the Negro. "The hard, cold fact of the matter is that the city's population has experienced a marked ethnic change and this change has had a decisive impact on the city's economic and social order." Mitchell reminded the commissioners that Newburgh had lost 4,075 whites and gained 3,098 Negroes during the last decade.

Accompanying this change we have lost many executives and higher-skilled type citizens and they have been replaced with low-skilled citizens. This has taken its toll in assessed valuations, business closings, bank mortgage policy, changes on financing based on the "spreading slum" theory, enormous school problems involving overcrowding and the need for costly classes in training the newcomers whose standards are below the permanent residents, and crime, disease, illegitimacy reflecting in other parts of the community. . . .

[The statement maintained that Newburgh welcomed] all newcomers, of any race. We shall treat all persons equally, be they Scotch, such as myself, or, in the words of Councilman George McKneally, "be they Irish Catholic" such as he. But newcomers have no right to wreck our city. They have no right to prejudice the interest of our citizens.

Describing his city to the board members, City Manager Mitchell contended:

Its employment situation is good and we have found that anyone who wants work can find it.[3] . . . For our present situation, however, where we have experienced a significant ethnic shift in population within the city, the lack of a broad base of unskilled labor jobs is a key factor in our problems. Our feeling is that we have reached a saturation point of unskilled labor. . . . We wish to keep our future bright, and to do this we must take actions on all social and economic fronts.

Portions of Mitchell's statement were published by the area press on the day of the hearing, but he did not get a chance to read it before the board members. Only one Newburgh official testified, Welfare Commissioner O'Donnell, and his statement had predictable, but unfortunate consequences.

The hearing took place in a meeting room in the lofty

[3] Mitchell consistently ignored the Federal Government's designation of the area as one "of substantial labor surplus."

State Office Building. At the rear sat the five members of the board who were conducting the hearing. In front of them, on their left, sat representatives of the city. On their right were members of the staff of the Department of Social Welfare. About seventy spectators were in the room, including members of the press, representatives of Gov. Rockefeller's staff, a joint committee of the New York legislature which had investigated welfare in 1960, members of the New York Mayors Conference (of which Bill Ryan was head), and representatives of the Empire State Chamber of Commerce.

Under the rules of procedure, outlined at the beginning of the session by Felix Infausto, welfare board counsel and secretary, testimony would be limited to the legality of the thirteen points.

Antonio A. Sorieri, deputy commissioner of welfare, was the first witness to be called by Infausto. Mr. Sorieri quoted sections of the state social welfare law which established the department's legal right to require minimum welfare regulations of the districts under it.

The next person to testify was Clifford P. Tallcott, area welfare director, whose sharp letter to Mitchell over the May muster had first attracted the attention of the Associated Press. He testified briefly about his attempts and failure to obtain a copy of a promised directive which would order the city's revolutionary program to be put into effect.

Bryon T. Hipple, Jr., deputy commissioner of administrative finance and statistics, followed. He sketched the federal aid program in the state and pointed out that the failure of any one district to comply with federal law could cut New York from all welfare aid from Washington.

It wasn't until William H. Kaufman, senior research analyst, took the stand as the welfare department's last witness that the newsmen present had material for a story. Kaufman's statistics belittled some of the chief arguments Mitchell had used to justify imposing the tough welfare policy.

To the City Manager's charge that "migrant types" from the South were replacing an excessive burden on the city, he answered that other cities with smaller percentages of Negroes had proportionally more persons on relief. Kaufman cited Oswego, another upstate city with its own welfare district, which had 42 persons per thousand on welfare compared to 29.1 per thousand in Newburgh. Yet Oswego's Negroes represented only .1 per cent of the population, compared to Newburgh's colored population of 16.6 per cent. Of the five New York cities of comparable size[4] which have their own welfare districts, Newburgh had the lowest proportion of public welfare recipients. Poughkeepsie, on the other side of the Hudson, had 31.4 welfare recipients per thousand; Jamestown, 31.6; and Auburn, 38.2. Oswego was fifth.

Further, Kaufman pointed out that in the last two years Newburgh had paid the almost unbelievably small total of $305 in relief to persons who had been in the city less than a year. "The only fair inference that could be drawn is that practically no unemployed newcomers to the state have received assistance from the City of Newburgh during the past two years," he told the committee.

Kaufman noted that when the number of persons on home relief exceeds 1 per cent of the community's population, the percentage of state aid rises from the usual 50 per cent to 80 per cent. He observed that although forty-one of the sixty-five welfare districts in the state received such extra aid, Newburgh was not among them, since at no time during

[4] Cities with a population range of 22,000 to 42,000.

1960 did the number of home-relief[5] recipients in the city exceed one per cent.

At least one of the city's economy-motivated thirteen points would cost the community more if enforced, the research analyst demonstrated. He referred to point thirteen which would remove the child from its parents' care if the environment was "not satisfactory." A welfare child cared for in his home cost Newburgh taxpayers an average of $5.90 monthly, Kaufman testified. Cared for in a foster home, the child cost the city an average of $37.50 per month, more than six times as much.

Nevertheless, as was testified later in the hearing, New York law, as in most other states, requires the welfare caseworker to safeguard the health and morals of a child by removing him from his home, if necessary. In most states, including New York, such drastic action may only be taken through court action in which concrete proof of neglect is shown, directives of a city's political head notwithstanding.

Kaufman's testimony knocked some of the underpinnings out from under the city's argument, but it lacked the interest of a dramatic struggle unwillingly provided by the next witness, Commissioner O'Donnell.

The 53-year-old welfare administrator found himself faced with a dilemma. He could state that he supported the new regulations, thereby displeasing the state Department of Social Welfare under whose regulations he would have to work if the city lost its fight; or he could declare opposition to the thirteen points, thereby offending the City Manager and the majority of the City Council, his imme-

[5] Generally, home relief covers needy persons not included in other welfare categories. Called general assistance in many states, it includes families whose unemployment benefits have been exhausted or whose salaries are not enough to maintain their families.

diate superiors. As O'Donnell was sworn in, it was obvious to everyone in the hearing room that he was ill at ease. His face was flushed and drawn. He fidgeted in his chair and wiped his sweating brow frequently with a handkerchief.

O'Donnell's testimony came as a grim surprise for the Mitchell-McKneally clique. He chose to acknowledge what those who knew him believed to be his honest position—that he didn't believe he was legally empowered to carry out the city's proposed welfare restrictions. But the admission did not slip out easily. It was drawn out of him by Infausto during an hour and one-half of probing questioning. One by one the Board's counsel went down the list of Newburgh's proposed welfare regulations asking O'Donnell to cite provisions in state law which would permit them to go into effect. Inevitably, the Commissioner was forced to answer that he didn't believe he could enforce them.

The official transcript of the hearing shows the line of questioning and the replies. A sample:

> *Infausto:* With respect to item four of the City Manager's directive to you, Commissioner—maybe you had better read it aloud.
>
> *O'Donnell:* [Reading] "All mothers of illegitimate children are to be advised that should they have any more children out of wedlock, they shall be denied relief."
>
> *Infausto:* Do you know of any provision of law which authorizes you to do that, Commissioner?
>
> *O'Donnell:* No, I do not, sir.
>
> *Infausto:* As a matter of fact, you are required, are you not, by the social welfare law to provide assistance for people in need so long as they are in need?
>
> *O'Donnell:* That is correct.
>
> *Infausto:* Regardless of the number of children they have, legitimate or otherwise?

O'Donnell: That is correct.

Infausto: So that it would be impossible for you to implement item four in the City Manager's directive lawfully. Is
that correct?

O'Donnell: Yes, sir.

The Welfare Commissioner testified that in his judgement
the law would not allow widespread use of vouchers instead
of cash. He acknowledged that if a man quit a job because
it was hazardous or injurious to his health, he could not
lawfully deny him assistance. And, he offered his belief that
a woman would not produce a child solely to get the $19 or
$20 in monthly relief benefits she might receive.

When it was over, Infausto congratulated O'Donnell on
the "frankness" of his testimony. "I think the committee
owes him a vote of thanks," he observed.

The Newburgh Welfare Commissioner was the last person to be called during the morning session. When it ad-
journed for lunch the city administration's case had been
expertly undermined. Mitchell's anger and frustration can
be judged by his later description of the hearing: "Communist show trial conductors could learn a lesson from the
writers, stage hands, actors, producers, and directors of this
one-act farce. The only thing it lacked to make it ready for
Boston testing prior to going on the New York stage was a
musical score."

The afternoon session blew up in dramatic discord twenty-
five minutes after it got underway. There was no testimony
supporting the city's legal claims to enforce the thirteen
points, and Mitchell never got a chance to read the lengthy
statement he had given to the press. The hearing collapsed
after Infausto said he found it pointless to examine the city
officials since they had not furnished any material showing
how they could carry out the thirteen points. "It seems to me

that there has been more than ample time, if these people
were honest, to deliver the material for us to examine today," he told the board members.

Mitchell chose this time to demand a right to speak.

"Do you wish to testify with respect to the legality of the
thirteen items that you have directed to the Commissioner
of Public Welfare of the City of Newburgh?" Chairman
Amend inquired.

The transcript records the verbal battle which followed
Amend's question:

> *Mitchell:* I have answers to this, but I would like to know
> if this board wishes to know the Newburgh situation.
>
> *Chairman Amend:* This committee is addressing itself to-
> day to the thirteen points contained in your directions to
> the Commissioner of Public Welfare of the City of New-
> burgh. If you wish to testify with respect to these thirteen
> points, you will be sworn, and you can testify. We are not
> going to hear any statements with respect to any other state-
> ments at this time.
>
> *Mitchell:* You mean you deny me the opportunity to
> make a statement?
>
> [At this, Infausto jumped from his chair and strode to-
> ward Mitchell.]
>
> *Infausto:* I object! You were told at the beginning of this
> inquiry that questions and answers would be asked pertain-
> ing to the legality of the thirteen points. You love publicity.
> You were addressing yourself to the press.
>
> [Councilman Doulin leaped to his feet.]
>
> *Doulin:* Sir!
>
> *Chairman Amend:* May I ask you to be seated until I
> have responded to Mr. Mitchell's statement. [Doulin sat
> down.] Mr. Mitchell, may I ask you, do you wish to testify
> with respect to the thirteen points in your directive to the
> city Commissioner?

> *Mitchell:* I wish to explain the Newburgh situation.
>
> *Chairman Amend:* Could you answer the question categorically? It is susceptible to a yes or no answer. Do you wish to testify on the matters that are relevant to today's hearing, namely, the thirteen points of your directive?
>
> *Mitchell:* That is what we came up for.
>
> *Chairman Amend:* Are you willing to testify and confine yourselves to those issues today?
>
> *Mitchell:* No.
>
> *Infausto:* I move that this hearing be adjourned.
>
> *Chairman Amend:* Mr. Doulin, did you wish to make a statement?
>
> *Doulin:* I just wanted to get one thing clear. The attorney said we were dishonest.
>
> *Infausto:* That is my opinion about not delivering this thing on time.
>
> *Doulin:* That is your opinion, that we are dishonest?
>
> *Infausto:* In that respect. I am not a politician.

It was Henry Hirschberg, the city's special counsel in the welfare battle, an 82-year-old quick-witted veteran of many a top courtroom battle, who gave the final answer of Mitchell-McKneally coterie minutes later. "We feel, in view of the limitation in connection with the testimony, if it is to be taken, that there is no purpose at this time that would be served by the witnesses that are subpoenaed testifying and taking up the time of the committee."

Mitchell and the majority of city fathers were not to be cowed by statistics. They left as unsubmissive as when they arrived. Attorney Hirschberg relayed the city administration's defiant message to the board members: Newburgh intended to enforce its thirteen points as scheduled on July 15. Infausto replied,

> In view of that, it seems to me that there would be little

purpose in holding further hearings. . . . My recommendation would be to hold a special meeting of the board and make a report to it of the situation. I would further recommend, . . . that the board issue a directive to the City of Newburgh officials not to implement, in which case, we will wind up in the courts. If that is what they want, let's get it over with.

The Newburgh officials returned home that night. The following day O'Donnell mailed his resignation to Mitchell. In character with its author its tone was mild, almost apologetic. O'Donnell wrote:

You have stated that as of July 15 the newly proposed program will become effective in the administration of welfare for the City of Newburgh. In the situation thus created, I find myself in the impossible position of being employed by the City of Newburgh to administer a program at variance with state law which I, by oath of office, have sworn to uphold.

Under these unfortunate circumstances, I cannot in all conscience carry on the work of this office. Therefore, I have no alternative except to submit my resignation effective immediately.

To some opponents of the Newburgh program O'Donnell was viewed as a hero. The New York State Public Welfare Association honored him with a citation "for his display of courage for principles that have withstood temporary assault and controversy. . . ." Commissioner Amend termed him "a man of great courage who told the truth about Newburgh."

If only that were true perhaps there would not have been a Newburgh controversy. For whatever O'Donnell's attributes, his greatest lack was courage. While the national news media was quoting the specious Citizens' Welfare

Study to explain Newburgh's problems, he remained silent about its true author. While millions were being told the majority of the city's recipients were Negro, O'Donnell, who had the correct figures on his desk, remained silent. While the city administration was castigating relief recipients as immoral, court problems, producers of disease and urban blight, O'Donnell made no attempt to defend them. When the welfare muster was held, O'Donnell, one of the few persons who knew of its planning and who signed the order, had no comment. O'Donnell, a civil service appointee, could have remained as commissioner and battled the city administration. His resignation was not an act of courage, but one of weakness and fear.

Mitchell, on receiving the resignation, publicly said he regretted the action of the Commissioner. Later, he attempted to discredit O'Donnell's testimony by contending he had been "carefully rehearsed" by the state Department of Welfare.

On July 12, state Welfare Commissioner Houston, at the direction of the executive committee of the state Board of Welfare, ordered the city not to put its welfare regulations into effect. Mitchell defiantly retorted once again that the regulations were within the law. He vowed they would be put in force on July 15 as planned, "regardless of demands." Commented the City Manager acidly:

> Mr. Houston is not the boss of the City of Newburgh, much as he may want to be or appear to be. We resent being ordered around by state officials who don't represent the interest of the taxpayers. We don't intend to honor his demands.

The stage was set for a court battle, and what Mitchell termed a "show trial" would play its last act in Newburgh.

EIGHT · "I'LL LEAVE IT UP TO THE LORD TO PROVIDE."

▼▼▼

ALMOST FORGOTTEN while the city and state powers wrangled over legalities, while welfare officials worried about the loss of federal aid, and while newspapers talked about home rule, were the men, women, and children dependent upon Newburgh's begrudging charity.

Of the 915 persons on relief, approximately half, 466, were children.[1] Another 246 were over sixty-five. Seventy-two persons were disabled and three were blind. The remaining 128 adults were mainly mothers receiving aid to dependent children for support of their families.[2]

I talked to many of them, often walking up unlighted and bannisterless stairs lined by grimy walls on which the paint was flaked and peeling, to dingy, overcrowded flats heated by ancient and dangerous-looking oil stoves. In the waterfront section where many of the reliefers live, it was not uncommon to see a line of children or adults buying fuel oil, a gallon or two at a time, from a tank truck parked on the street.

[1] Of the 466 children, ninety were illegitimate.
[2] On the national level roughly the same exists. Of the 8,300,000 persons on the welfare rolls in 1965, about 40 per cent were children, 30 per cent were aged, 6 per cent disabled, 1 per cent blind, and the remaining 13 per cent able-bodied adults.

Contrary to the stories being spread about relief recipients driving to City Hall in big cars, spending all their money on booze, and owning expensive television sets, the welfare families I visited were truly destitute. A 57-year-old Negro woman in a city housing project was about to sit down to her main meal of the day when I visited her unexpectedly. The meal consisted of fried potatoes mixed with fat, and coffee. For breakfast, she told me, she had eaten a few slices of bread and had drunk some more coffee. A 29-year-old Negro mother cared for her nine children—three of whom were illegitimate—in a dreary, dim, 3½-room apartment.

They were not the exceptions; most welfare families live under conditions the middle-class suburbanite would think unendurable and sickening. The average person, if he had a choice, would not lively solely on welfare checks. To qualify, in most states, he would have to give up his car, his house, sign over his insurance policies, and feed and clothe each of his children on slightly more than a dollar a day. In New York, which has one of the most liberal welfare policies in the nation, general relief payments to a single person for food, clothing, transportation, toilet supplies, and other incidentals per month can run as high as $39.35 if the individual is unemployed, to $53.55 for a man employed at heavy work receiving insufficient income. In 1961 the average payment to Newburgh mothers to care for their children was $20.50 monthly.

Always, when I interviewed welfare recipients, I found them eager to tell their troubles. Always, they said they preferred work to charity. In the majority of cases the likelihood of their working was slim. The welfare rolls are heavily loaded with the disabled, the incompetent, the unskilled, the uneducated, and the untrainable. Not everyone can be a winner in a competitive society. These are the worst losers.

There are cheats, persons who are surreptitiously working at well-paying jobs or receiving other benefits while accepting public assistance, but, contrary to common belief, in the nation their numbers are few in comparison with the numbers legally receiving assistance. A recent survey conducted by the Department of Health, Education, and Welfare disclosed that in thirty-four states suspected chiseling involved less than 2 per cent of the welfare recipients. The highest chiseling rate was 7.4 per cent in Delaware and Nevada.

Another prevalent attitude I found among welfare recipients is best summed up in the shopworn phrase of the downtrodden, "You can't fight City Hall." But it was stated in a tone which expressed not a feeling of despair, but a hopeful belief that everything would turn out all right in the end.

"I wouldn't know what to do if my relief were cut off," Mrs. Arnold, a disheveled, white, ADC mother in her early forties, told me as I talked to her in the kitchen of her cluttered flat. Paint was peeling off the wall of one of the five rented rooms. Dirty dishes were in the sink and on the table. Faded and patched clothing hung from a line strung in the center of the room. She explained she works on and off in the pocketbook factories, but because of her "bad eyes" is usually the first to be laid off when work is slow. A pair of thick-lensed glasses magnified her eyes out of proportion to the rest of her narrow face, giving her the appearance of a bewildered owl.

Rent for the apartment was $45 a month. She accused her landlady of taking advantage of her being on welfare. The woman next door, she claimed, was paying $10 less, and had a better apartment.

Welfare supports Mrs. Arnold and her three children,

aged thirteen, eight, and six, on $166 monthly, in addition to paying the rent for her apartment. She is separated from her husband, a truck driver who pays her $40 weekly toward support of her family when he has a job. Just then, he was not working, and so contributed nothing. Whenever her husband is employed the welfare department drops the family from its rolls. "I don't really approve of welfare if you could help it," she told me.

The family had been on and off relief for four years when I talked to her. "They don't give you enough to help out," she said of the money received from the welfare department. "I haven't bought no clothing of any kind in six months." The children go without milk because, Mrs. Arnold says, the relief check is not big enough for her to afford fresh milk.

I asked her where she was born. "New Windsor," she replied, naming a residential suburb just outside of the city.

"When did you come to Newburgh?"

"When I was twenty-one, right after I got married."

"How long ago was that?"

"About twenty years ago."

Another migrant, I thought, remembering Mitchell's definition of the term.

Contrasting with Mrs. Arnold's untidy apartment was one kept by Mrs. Elaine Disnuke, who, with her son and daughter, occupies a 3½-room apartment in a city housing project on the waterfront. A dwarf, slightly more than four feet tall as the result of crippling rheumatoid arthritis, Mrs. Disnuke's apartment was nevertheless spotless and cheerful when I visited it unexpectedly. Unable to buy slip covers to put over the worn, second-hand furniture in the apartment, the 33-year-old mother had fashioned her own covers from bright, flower-printed drapes given to her. Water colors had been applied to the living room rug in a temporary effort to restore the color to its faded surface.

Mrs. Disnuke's husband walked out on her in 1954 leaving her to attempt to support a three-year-old daughter and a one-year-old son. In 1962 he was discovered in neighboring Poughkeepsie and Mitchell had him jailed for non-support. The imprisonment of her husband has had no effect on Mrs. Disnuke's living standards. Welfare continues to pay her utilities and her monthly rent of $56.50, in addition to $46.75 every thirty days to support her and her children.

Mrs. Disnuke, a light-skinned Negress whose long dark hair and heavy, black eyebrows make her look Middle Eastern rather than Negroid, is proud of her children. Both appeared to be shy, well-behaved youngsters during the only time I saw them. She is especially proud of her daughter who in the fall of 1965 was attending accelerated classes in junior high school after having been on the honor roll throughout her years in grade school. If the girl continues on her scholarly path she has an excellent chance of winning a college scholarship.

Because of her concern for her children, Mrs. Disnuke would like to get off welfare. "I'd like to get a job because I don't want the children to think you can get something for nothing. They have to learn you have to make a living by the sweat of your brow," she told me. In an effort to make herself employable, she has learned typing and bookkeeping. But no one in Newburgh has offered her a permanent job. Still optimistic that someone will hire her, she keeps a battered old typewriter in her apartment on which she practices regularly to maintain her skill. In September 1964 she sent a letter to local businesses asking for jobs she could do at home. In response, she received a temporary job doing minor typewriting in her apartment. It paid $3.00 a month. The law required that her welfare check be decreased by the same amount.

When I saw her last in the summer of 1965 the job had ended and she was still doggedly looking for employment. While she waits, Mrs. Disnuke, despite her disability, keeps more active in civic work than any two suburban house-wives. She is recording secretary for her son's school parent-teacher association and has been district captain of the Cancer Fund Drive and Heart Fund as well as a volunteer worker for the March of Dimes.

A Baptist, Mrs. Disnuke directed her church's Vacation Bible School for four years, taught religious courses during public school release time and played the organ of the Ulster County Migrant Chapel. Her interest in the migrants resulted in her being named a director of the Ulster County Migrant Committee.

Her other non-paid activities included being a Cub Scout den mother, founding and editing a ten-page newspaper for tenants in the housing project and serving on the lay advisory committee of a predominantly Negro public grade school. Artistically inclined, Mrs. Disnuke spends much of her remaining time making posters for school and other community groups or fashioning animals out of odds and ends.

Admittedly, Mrs. Disnuke and her children are not examples of typical welfare recipients. But neither are the highly-publicized cases of abuse such as the New Jersey family which collected $969 monthly in relief checks, or the Texas man who picked up four cases of surplus relief food and drove away in an air-conditioned Cadillac.

Two floors above Mrs. Disnuke's living quarters I knocked on the door of an apartment kept by a 63-year-old grandmother. Upon being admitted I walked into a living room which, like the one on the lower floor, showed evidence of having been swept and dusted recently. A worn, upholstered chair and a matching davenport from which cotton stuffing blossomed in patches were near the door. A use-scratched wooden table, bearing cigarette burns and ring-shaped discolorations, and four wooden chairs occupied a place near a window overlooking a parking lot. An ancient upright piano losing its top layer of yellow paint was against one wall of the living room. Half of the ivory was off the keys and (I later learned) at least a third of them no longer worked.

"I saved it when they were going to throw it away," the grandmother explained when I remarked about the instrument. "My granddaughter wants to learn on the piano."

The parents of the granddaughter were alive but were reported to be unable to support the girl. She was one of two teenagers who lived in the apartment. The other was the white-haired Negress's 19-year-old son who worked three days a week in a pocketbook factory for $1.15 an hour. His check, after deductions, amounted to approximately $20 weekly. The money was not enough to support them. The chances are that the young man will never earn much more than the minimum wage. He dropped out of school after the sixth grade.

The grandmother was slightly built and her skin was brown and wrinkled, like the outside of a spoiled peach. Her movements were the brittle and measured labors of the aged.

"I'd work if I could," she explained to me. "I used to work—do housekeeping. I can't no more. I got heart trouble. I don't think people who can work should be on relief. Lord knows I wouldn't be on it if I could help it."

Her monthly welfare check totaled $103. She said the three of them barely managed to "get by" each month. "I pay $56.50 rent for this apartment. It used to be cheaper when I first moved here. That was . . . about four years ago."

The old woman had been on relief since 1952 when she came to Newburgh from the city of Beacon, directly across the Hudson, with her family. At that time it included another son and a daughter, now married and the mother of the 13-year-old girl.

Why did they come to Newburgh?

"We couldn't find no fit place to live on the other side of the river."

The aged Negress and her husband, who had died the year before the family came to Newburgh, arrived in New York in 1924 after leaving North Carolina. "We heard tell things were better up North," she explained. The living was tougher than they expected. But, she would never return to the South.

"Have you heard of the city's new welfare code?" I asked.

"Yes, I heard something about it. But I'm not going to worry about it none. The Lord's taken care of me so far. I'll leave it up to the Lord to provide. I'm not going to worry about it."

Not all the city welfare recipients looked upon Mitchell's welfare crusade as stoically. In mid-July, just after the thirteen points went into effect a local social worker told a newsman:

If Mr. Mitchell thinks his program has been psychologically successful on frauds, then he'd better take another look at the welfare situation. An 83-year-old woman, a widow of one of Newburgh's most prominent citizens, walked several miles to the welfare office with every one of the newspaper clippings on the welfare mess.

"How long have I got before they turn me out?" she asked me. I tried to assure her that the new rules don't affect old age assistance. But when she left the office she was still weeping. Is this the kind of psychological effect Mitchell wants?

Another woman is on her way to Middletown State Hospital for the Insane. She is wild and inconsolable. She's sure that they'll throw her out into the street.

According to the caseworker's account little sympathy was expressed by Mitchell toward the plight of the unfortunate. "One of our caseworkers went up to him about a particularly bad case. You knew what he said when she was all through?

" 'Stop acting like a damn writer for *The Ladies Home Journal.' "[3]

His lack of concern was not shared by the state Department of Welfare. On July 14, the day before the thirteen points were to take effect, the department sent five staff members into the city to check on all home-relief and aid-to-dependent-children cases. Their instructions were to examine each case to see that the state welfare regulations and standards were met. Any variance with what the state interpreted to be the welfare law or any attempt to enforce any of the thirteen regulations would be reported, Commissioner Houston promised.

"Gestapo agents," Mitchell called them.

On the same day Governor Nelson A. Rockefeller revealed at a news conference that he was opposed to the Newburgh plan. He raised the possibility of removing city officials if they went ahead to put the program in force. "The Governor has the authority and power to remove local governments from office" if they violate the law, he reminded newsmen.

July 15 was a Saturday. Although the Newburgh welfare

[3] *Middletown Times Herald-Record,* July 18, 1961.

Mitchell talks the situation over in his office with (l-r) Special
Counsel Henry Hirschberg, Acting Welfare Commissioner Doris
Harding, and Corporation Counsel Lawrence Herbst. This was
on July 19, two days after the fiasco of the 13-point implementation. Although everyone is smiling, the presence of the two
lawyers is an indication of the seriousness of the just-beginning
injunction proceedings by the State of New York.

112 THE DESPISED POOR

office was closed for the weekend, Mitchell issued an order to Mrs. Doris B. Harding, who was acting welfare commissioner in the absence of O'Donnell, directing her to refer all ADC cases and home-relief cases to the corporation counsel's office. She was also asked to require all able-bodied males to report to City Hall before being assigned to work-relief projects.

Because of the weekend she decided to wait until Monday before taking any action. Mitchell himself was in Washington, D.C. addressing a meeting of the conservative Human Events Conference.

On Monday, July 17, the City Manager arrived in his City Hall office to find a new migrant-worker problem on his hands—newsmen from nearly all sections of the nation were in town waiting for a dramatic enforcement of the thirteen points.

A CBS crew, filming a special half-hour documentary on the controversy, filled Mitchell's office with flood lights, sound equipment, and cameras. Outside City Hall, an ABC camera team set up its equipment. The strategic location of its equipment virtually gave CBS first rights to film Mr. Mitchell, but as its crew changed film or readjusted the lights, ABC would rush in and bring the City Manager outside to be filmed for its show.

Two other camera crews, one from Movietone News, the other from an Albany television station, filmed Newburgh's chief administrator when no one else had a lens aimed at him. And, when no one was televising Mr. Mitchell, reporters questioned him anywhere they could find him—on his City Hall balcony, in his office, or on the City Hall steps.

At the same time, other reporters and photographers were clustered around Mrs. Harding and around the observers sent to Newburgh by the state. While all this was happening, Mayor Ryan called a press conference in his office which drew more photographers. The only element missing was a *Life* reporter-photographer team. That didn't show up until Tuesday.

Unfortunately for Mr. Mitchell, the day turned out to be a fiasco. Most of the thirteen points could not be implemented immediately, since they called for time-consuming review of cases. Even denial of relief would have no effect until the welfare checks' scheduled delivery of August 1. And there were no illegitimate children born that day.

Work relief, however, could be put into effect simply by asking those available to report to City Hall where they could be assigned duties. The fact that the building was crawling with reporters, photographers, and cameramen was incidental.

Earlier in the summer Mitchell had estimated that the number of men on relief eligible for work projects might run as high as sixty. Mayor Ryan had retorted that the City Manager would find no more than six. Welfare officials scoured the relief rolls for eligible males. They came up with three names. One was discovered to have private employment, but was not earning enough to support his family. He was dropped from the list. The remaining two were ordered to City Hall. There, photographers snapped their pictures as they were interviewed by a pleasant young woman, Mrs. Evelyn Napolitano, who filled the dual role of secretary to both the police chief and the local Civil Service Commission.

One of the pair, a 45-year-old Negro porter, was discovered to be a cripple. His name was scratched. The second, a 33-year-old white iron worker with one eye, was the father of five children under nine. A check with the hospital later confirmed his story that his pregnant wife was a patient there suffering from a lung disease. He was permitted to return home to look after the children.

Undaunted, despite his failure to find a single able-bodied man on the relief rolls ineligible for relief, Mitchell faced newsmen and the cameras. The publicity given his stringent welfare program had frightened the loafers into dropping off the relief rolls, he told them.[4]

In view of Mitchell's remarkable lack of success in finding either frauds or idlers, it was maddening to read a *New York Daily News* editorial in August 1962 which suggested a medal should be given the City Manager for "booting chiselers and deadbeats off his relief rolls" some thirteen months before. At the time of publication of the editorial, Mitchell had yet to prove a single chiseling case and the vaunted work relief program had proven to be a dud.

[4] Yet the records showed that there were no work-reliefers working for the city the previous July. However, in June 1960 one man was employed for four days cutting the lawn on city-owned properties.

NINE · INJUNCTION

❦❦❦❦❦❦❦❦❦❦❦❦❦❦❦❦❦❦❦❦❦❦❦❦❦❦❦❦❦❦❦❦❦❦❦❦

ONCE MITCHELL HAD DISOBEYED Commissioner Houston's order against putting the thirteen points into effect, the state Board of Social Welfare acted swiftly. On July 18, at its monthly meeting held in Saranac Lake, New York, the board requested New York State Attorney General Louis J. Lefkowitz to take action to block the carrying out of the welfare program.

At the same time it released a blistering statement attacking Mitchell and his political backers which in part said:

> In the light of the facts, we find no justification whatever for the measures Newburgh proposes to adopt. . . .
>
> We especially deplore the spectacle of public officials threatening to violate the laws they swore to administer, and publicizing the program of violation they intend to carry out, and [we deplore] the devices they propose to use to deny certain citizens their constitutional rights—and receiving encouragment and support from some sources. . . .
>
> Every citizen has a right to seek changes in the laws. No citizen, however, has the right to encourage or advocate breaking the law.

The board's request to take legal steps against the program was, in effect, a directive placing Lefkowitz, a Republican, in a difficult position. As New York Attorney General he was obliged to carry out the demand of the state body. Yet he was about to run for the New York City mayorality against the politically-powerful Democratic incumbent Robert F. Wagner.

The Republican candidate was well aware that a large slice of the populace in New York City, as elsewhere in the nation, was in sympathy with Newburgh and its tough welfare program. More than half the city newspapers backed Mitchell. To take a strong stand would injure his already slim chances of winning.[1]

He responded to the poltical problem by restricting his public comments to the legal role his office would now have to take. In his first public statement he indicated considerable efforts were being made to persuade him to take no action against Newburgh. Lefkowitz told the press in a prepared statement on July 21,

> Letters, telegrams and telephone calls received by me have indicated that there is a public misunderstanding as to my role as the attorney general in the Newburgh welfare situation.
>
> Under the law I must provide legal advice and assistance to every state agency requesting same. . . . I have nothing at all to do with the policy underlying the enactment of any welfare law or regulation adopted by the federal, state or local unit of government. I am acting in a legal capacity only. As chief legal officer of the State, I am compelled to

---

[1] One announced candidate for the New York City mayoralty post, New York City Controller Lawrence E. Gerosa, announced on July 23, as Lefkowitz's office was preparing for its coming court battle with Newburgh, that he might adopt at least some of the thirteen points if he were elected. "I would examine the plan and if it would work in New York, I'd put it in," he told a local television audience. In the election, Gerosa ran far behind both other candidates.

refrain from expressing my personal views when I am called upon to determine the question of legality.

The impression the Attorney General seemed to be trying to create was that he was being forced into moving against the Newburgh program. Lefkowitz further divorced himself from the controversy by appointing state Solicitor General Paxton Blair to do the legal fighting.

The choice was a logical and good one. Blair could not match Hirschberg's sixty-one years of legal practice, but he had been a lawyer for forty-three years and was a former member of the state welfare board. At sixty-eight, the Solicitor General had been in private practice and had also served in the New York City corporation counsel's office under Mayor Fiorello H. LaGuardia. Shortly afterward, he was appointed to fill an unexpired term on the New York State Supreme Court. The term lasted only a few months, but it earned him the permanent title of judge.

With his thick, white hair parted in the middle, white mustache, and well-dressed appearance, he looked every inch the Hollywood stereotyped judge. An AP reporter described Judge Blair as having "an old-world manner and an air of legal dignity." A slight southern accent reminded those who knew of his past that he had been born in New Orleans.

Despite the appointment of Blair to pursue the Newburgh case, Lefkowitz had not abandoned hope of avoiding an open court battle between the city and state, which could very likely be injurious to both himself and Rockefeller, then coming up for reelection in a year. On July 24 the Attorney General and Blair met in Albany behind closed doors with Mitchell, Hirschberg, and Corporation Counsel Lawrence Herbst to confer on the situation.

Lefkowitz was unable to reach any compromise with the

Mitchell-McKneally power group, and on July 28 he asked
the state supreme court to issue a temporary injunction forbidding the city from enforcing twelve of the thirteen
points. The exception was point ten which required welfare
recipients not blind, disabled, or ill to report monthly to the
Newburgh Department of Public Welfare for a conference
on the status of their cases. That point, the state admitted,
was legal.

Included among the papers was an affidavit by one of
those Mitchell termed a "Gestapo agent," Miss Marie C.
Murray, state senior welfare representative and a member
of the team of observers sent to Newburgh to determine
whether the city was carrying out its threatened welfare
program.

Miss Murray, a gray-haired, motherly-looking woman in
her fifties who served in Europe during World War II as a
top Red Cross official, declared, "events have been repeatedly occurring in such a manner as to form a pattern of relief administration in accordance with the thirteen-point
program and to constitute strong and persuasive evidence of
a policy which is at variance with the policy of relief administration established by federal law, rules and regulations."

Repeated radio and newspaper announcements by city
officials boasting that a tough welfare program was in effect,
she swore, had intimidated some of the needy from applying
for relief for themselves or their children. In addition, she
said, letters were sent by Mitchell to all mothers of illegitimate
children advising them that if they had any more children out of wedlock, an investigation of their home environment would be made to see if the children should be placed
in foster homes.[2] The letters also advised the mothers to be-

[2] The letter was evidence that the city had changed its stated
position that the mothers would be denied all relief. On July 21

come self-supporting or face the possibility of being denied relief after three months.

Other than the actions cited by Miss Murray, few changes had been made in the operation of the welfare department in the two weeks since its "revolutionary" program had gone into effect. The trumpets on the city's welfare bandwagon were playing as loudly as before, but the bandwagon was barely moving. A family of seven, receiving a total of $60.27 monthly in welfare payments, had been put on vouchers, all able-bodied reliefers were ordered to pick up their checks in person at the welfare department, and the city's corporation counsel began a one-a-day review of a total of 151 welfare cases to see how the thirteen points applied to each. When members of the press pointed out that on the basis of five working days per week it would take more than thirty weeks to go through all the cases, Mitchell replied, "We are not interested in speed, but in care and deliberation. We don't have the staff, and we don't want to make a big show."

The city was still looking for someone to put on work relief.

On Friday, August 4, the courses the city and state powers were taking collided in a Newburgh court room as counsels for both sides argued over whether the temporary injunction should be granted.

The city's legal general, the fiery Hirschberg, declared he was willing to challenge the Federal Social Security Law in

---

Mitchell had told reporters, "What a woman does off public relief is between her conscience and the clergy. My point is that it's the taxpayers' money and I don't think the taxpayer should pay for illegitimacy."

Mitchell admitted that placing the children in foster homes "might be more expensive in a quick dollar outlay, but it will make better citizens of them."

the United States Supreme Court, if that action was necessary to show that most of Newburgh's program was in accordance with the law.

Believed to be the oldest practicing attorney in New York State at that time, the bantam Henry Hirschberg at eighty-two was regarded as one of the most wily and skillful lawyers in the Hudson Valley. He boasted of never having lost any of the more than a hundred murder cases he had argued either as attorney for the accused or as a prosecuting district attorney.

Hirschberg's independence as well as his popularity can be gauged by the fact that he won the post the first time in 1915 as an independent with Democratic endorsement, resigned after three years, then returned to politics in 1933 to win it back as a Republican, finally resigning six years later to defend a labor leader accused of embezzlement.[3]

A man deeply concerned with individual rights, Hirschberg was once described by Clarence Darrow as "probably the only humane district attorney in the nation." He said of his terms as district attorney, "I was haunted by the fear that I would convict an innocent man and it wouldn't be discovered until that man had served several years in jail."

When McKneally and Mitchell pleaded with the octogenarian lawyer in late June to defend the city's case, Hirschberg agreed as a matter of principle as much as anything else. First, the veteran attorney told me later, he thought

[3] Hirschberg's most important case before the welfare battle was in 1958 when he played a strikingly different role as the defense counsel for upstate industrialist Malcolm R. White, who was charged with the murder of Alfred R. Dugan, union organizer and reputed strong-arm man. White was acquitted of all charges although the prosecutor showed he fired seven shots at Dugan, the fatal one entering his back.

more power should be vested in local governments. Second, he said, "I believed in the thirteen points."

To those acquainted with Hirschberg, his belief in the thirteen points was consistent with his admitted reactionary side. He was a member of the National Association to Repeal the Income Tax, an organization to which he was fiercely loyal. And, although he witnessed the highly-successful water fluoridation test in Newburgh, he was a determined member of the Anti-Fluoridation League.

There may have been a third reason why Hirschberg was willing to argue the Newburgh administration's cause. In his sixty-one years before the bar, he had never argued a case before the United States Supreme Court. This case had legal aspects which might afford him that opportunity.

There was probably no building in the county more familiar to Hirschberg than the County Court House he was about to enter that sunny, early August day. As a young boy his family lived in the house across the street and he had witnessed his father, a former state Supreme Court justice, hearing cases from the bench. A colonial-style building of cream-painted brick and round white wooden pillars, the court house was built near the close of the last century. Curiously, it is one of the two county court houses in Orange County. The early residents were never able to reach an agreement on whether the court house should be built in the Village of Goshen in the center of the county, or in Newburgh, the county's largest city. As a result, they compromised and constructed a court house at each location. Terms of the County Court alternate between the two court houses.

Usually, when either County Court or state Supreme Court is in session in the second floor court room, only a few dozen persons can be found in or around the old Court House. Today, the court room was packed with spectators. Newsmen from the metropolitan papers and the wire services buttonholed the opposing counsels for statements and copies of their briefs. Television cameramen filmed interviews with city officials as they entered and left the building. And, on the sidewalk in front of the Court House, the elderly Charles V. Smith distributed copies of the race-baiting *Truth Seeker* until his arrest minutes before the hearing.

Present in the court room under subpoena were Mitchell, looking cheerful; Mayor Ryan; the Republican members of the City Council; Corporation Counsel Herbst; and a new figure in the controversy, newly-appointed city Welfare Commissioner Peter Z. Petrillo, Jr.

The handsome, sun-tanned Mr. Petrillo, appointed on July 28 to replace O'Donnell, had been commissioner hardly long enough to say ADC before he was handed a summons to appear at the hearing. A former college fullback, the biggest thrill in the 32-year-old commissioner's athletic career was when he ran sixty yards on fourth down to score the only touchdown in a game between Newburgh Free Academy and Middletown High School. Now with Newburgh again on fourth down, he was being asked to run with a political football.

"I chose Mr. Petrillo because he is philosophically in agreement with me and because I think he can do a capable job," Mitchell told the press on the morning he announced the appointment. The City Manager had sounded out the former athlete the evening before in the Mitchell home.

Mitchell revealed the kind of thinking he demanded of welfare department employees a week later when he announced that no caseworkers would be hired unless they were "in philosophical harmony" with the city administration's ideas toward government. Thereafter, he declared, the question of whether an applicant was hired would be determined by his viewpoint of the role of government in the United States society. "He will be asked his opinion of the role of private capital and the role of the individual in our governmental system," the City Manager announced. His answers, Mitchell indicated, would be a vital factor in determining whether the applicant would be hired.

"Thought control is what we're doing," he stated bluntly. He called his new program "a philosophical breakthrough." "The philosophy of a trained social worker is the opposite of our philosophy. They believe that society owes a duty to the individual. We believe that the individual owes a duty to society." When a caseworker left, according to Mitchell, he would be replaced by "someone whose philosophy is in harmony with our philosophy." What would be determined, he said, "is whether the person is an equalitarian of the socialistic variety." Asked to define an equalitarian, he answered, "An equalitarian is a socialist. He wants more government, more control, more spending, more taxes."

Mitchell, glowing with enthusiasm, continued to give examples of the type of questions which would be asked and the answers he expected. Applicants, he said, would be asked, "What is a [welfare] chiseler?"

"If they tell us someone legally unqualified to receive aid," he declared, "we will tell them they missed the question."

Petrillo doesn't recall any questions being asked about his philosophy during his interview with Mitchell. Nevertheless, the City Manager seemed to feel he had the right man.

Perhaps what influenced Mitchell most to appoint Petrillo was his almost complete lack of qualifying experience for the job. After a year at Brown University, to which he had received an athletic scholarship, a knee injury prompted him to quit school and become a construction worker. Encouraged by his father, then a Newburgh tavern owner, Petrillo enrolled in Ithaca College the following fall. There he starred as a fullback and linebacker on the varsity football team while majoring in physical education. At Ithaca Petrillo had his only previous contact with social work—as a part time recreation director at a settlement house.

After graduating from college in 1953 he received a job as an instructor in science and physical education at the New York Military Academy in nearby Cornwall. (Petrillo had attended NYMA, an exclusive military prep school, after graduating from Newburgh Free Academy in 1946.) He remained at the Academy for four years, then left to become physical education instructor in the Midland Park, New Jersey public school system. He stayed for three years, until returning to Cornwall to teach physical education to the town's elementary school pupils.

Thomas D. Shost, supervising principal of Cornwall Central Schools, said of Petrillo's work with the children, "Pete did an awfully good job. The kids loved him and he helped us out in football. We hated to see him go, but we got a local girl for the position."

At the end of June 1961 Petrillo's contract with the school board expired. He had no prospects of another teaching position. As he had during other school vacations, Petrillo went to work for his brother-in-law, Edward J. Pekar, the owner of a Newburgh service station.

The previous spring Petrillo, a Republican, had mentioned to Councilman McIntyre that he was looking for a job. In mid-July as Mitchell searched, without success, for someone to replace O'Donnell, Petrillo's name was mentioned to him. The fateful evening interview followed. Now, as he walked into the Orange County Court House with only a week of experience as a welfare commissioner to his credit, it was too early to decide how well he would perform in his new job.

What Petrillo saw when he entered the courtroom resembled a cross between the opening of a political convention and an impatient fight crowd waiting for the main bout. Reporters and radio newsmen filled the grand jury box at the left of the courtroom. Newspaper and television cameramen aimed their lenses at personalities in the corridors and on the Court House veranda. Mayor Ryan sat in the rear of the packed courtroom. The other members of the council sat clustered near Mitchell in the second and third rows.

It was hot and stuffy in the courtroom, and the spectators grew impatient as they waited while a grand jury handed in its indictments and a calendar of some thirty motions involving other cases was read. They talked among themselves and the buzzing caused the bailiff to tap loudly on the railing several times to bring a comparative degree of quiet into the courtroom. At one point Mitchell began reading a New York City tabloid he had carried into the Court House, but an attendant promptly asked him to put it down and he complied.

Finally, a few minutes before 11 A.M. the hearing began before Justice John P. Donahoe, who had been a children's court judge before being elevated to the State Supreme Court. It began with a minor development—the appearance of former Special County Court Judge Edward G. O'Neill on behalf of Mayor Ryan. Judge O'Neill, a Democrat, presented an affidavit to the court stating the mayor's opposition to the new welfare regulations.

The actions of the City Manager and the Republican members of the council were, according to the mayor's statement, "not only in large part illegal, but were unnecessary, inhumane and immoral and designed to intimidate needy persons from applying for public relief."

The mayor's affidavit was only the preface to the conflict of ideas between Blair and Hirschberg. As the first to argue his case, Blair singled out six of the thirteen points for special reference, declaring each illegal. They were: point one, calling for aid in voucher form; point four, involving mothers of illegitimate children; point six, specifying that family allotments not exceed the take-home pay of the lowest-paid city employee with a comparable family ("A city does not always pay its employees with a view to their needs," Blair declared.); point eight, requiring new applicants for relief to show they had come to the city in response to a job offer; and point nine, limiting aid to three months, except for the aged, blind, and disabled.

In his brief, Blair argued that

> the public concern over the Newburgh controversy reaches far beyond the plight of the Newburgh indigent. Every public welfare district of the State faces problems similar to those of Newburgh and is subject to the precise statutes, rules and regulations with respect to which the Newburgh plan is in conflict. . . . It is essential that the legal issues be resolved before Newburgh actually deprives the indigent members of the community of the food, shelter and medical care to which they would be entitled under State law.

Mr. Blair told the court that the possibility, held out to the poor, of hiring a lawyer and receiving a court judgement that they are receiving less than their due "is nothing more than a teasing illusion like a munificent bequest in a pauper's will. It is no remedy at all; it fails utterly to accomplish the objectives of the instant suit." It is enough to show, he said, that the rights of the members of society are endangered, threatened, or placed in uncertainty to invoke the aid of the court.

As Hirschberg rose and began speaking, it was evident that his skill and acumen had not been diminished one whit by age, and there was very little to suggest that his energy or physical powers were failing. His voice, rasping and sibilant, was still strong. He paced in front of the bench, his head thrown back, his thumbs hooked in the pockets of his vest, clicking off his arguments as though he were reading them high on the court room wall.

When he gestured, his hand made a quick jabbing motion toward the bench, then returned to his vest pocket. One was reminded that he had fought as an amateur featherweight while a young lawyer in New York City. His quick movements and energy gave the appearance of a man thirty years younger, and Hirschberg's appearance enforced that misconception. His full head of hair, though liberally streaked with gray, was not yet white. His face was lined, but not deeply etched, and although he wore rimless glasses, his eyesight was keen. Only in profile, when he tossed his head back, did one notice that the creases in his neck, like the top of an old tan leather shoe in appearance, seemed to go into the flesh itself.

Now as he paced the court room, he moved to dismiss the case on the ground that the city had not yet violated the state welfare law. "The mere passing of the resolution embodying the thirteen points or any direction to the city manager to enforce them would not warrant the extraordinary relief of injunction," he contended. He told the

court that as a matter of fact, there has been no enforcement of any of the thirteen points in any manner contrary to law.

Hirschberg further argued that a court injunction could
not be obtained, even if the city were guilty, because the
state hadn't used all its legal means to force compliance, and
that if the state had wished to forestall implementation of
the disputed program it could have withheld welfare funds.

The hearing was over by noon. As expected, Justice
Donahoe reserved decision until a later date. As he left
the Court House, McKneally told a reporter, "I am confident as to the eventual outcome in our favor."

Within ten days of the hearing, both sides filed supplemental briefs shoring up their arguments.

Hirschberg's brief, submitted on August 8, charged the
state Department of Welfare with ignoring the needs of the
community. He declared he felt from experience that

> the welfare department has not vigorously enforced the pro-
> visions of the present welfare act with broad reference to
> the good of the community as well as the aid of those actu-
> ally in need of aid. . . .
>
> Newburgh is suffering from a rapidly expanding slum
> area due, it is believed, in large part to failure to adequately
> enforce the welfare law and also to the failure to enact a
> one-year residential requirement such as surrounding states
> have. The city manager and the council are endeavoring so
> far as possible within the law to arrest this slum increase
> and deterioration of property.

Five day's later Blair submitted his second brief. In it
he replied to the city's challenge of the Federal Security Act:

> It is too late to challenge the existence of a power which
> has been exercised with wide public acceptance for a quar-

ter of a century and whose constitutionality seems to have been pretty clearly declared.

The Solicitor General's principal argument was directed against Hirschberg's motion to dismiss the injunction proceedings on the grounds that the state had the alternative of notifying the city it was cutting off state funds. Blair asserted that if state aid were withheld, two things would happen: The plight of the poor would be "appallingly worsened," and the situation could only be remedied by increasing the tax burden on the citizens of Newburgh.

"It should be manifest that the relief we seek will impose a lesser hardship on Newburgh than the alternatives put forward by its own counsel," asserted the Solicitor General.

On August 18 Justice Donahoe announced his decision: The temporary injunction was granted!

"It sufficiently appears to this court," the jurist said, "that the defendants have chosen to trespass in an area which the legislature has reserved for the agencies charged with the responsibility of carrying out the welfare policies and programs of the state."

Mitchell commented: "This was expected. We shall appeal. In the meantime, we shall continue our other measures which are showing promise of being just as effective as the thirteen points."

Asked to describe the "other measures" to which he was referring, Mitchell said he meant such things as reorganization of the welfare department and the hiring of new personnel—an apparent reference to his announced policy of hiring caseworkers "in philosophical harmony" with him. He also meant, he said, a recent requirement under which adults receiving welfare checks were being forced to appear at the welfare building in order to be photographed.

Boasted the City Manager: "The only way the state Board of Social Welfare and the Attorney General can stop our welfare program will be to take over the operation of the welfare department or remove us from office." Perhaps so, but the board could spike the thirteen points. On December 19, following a hearing before state Supreme Court Justice Robert Doscher two weeks before, the state was granted a permanent injunction halting Newburgh's welfare program.

In his decision, Justice Doscher found that "the clear, unambiguous language" of the thirteen points itself violated both state and federal laws. No more proof was required, he observed, "than the defendant's defense wherein an attempt has been made to turn aside the onus [of violating the state and federal law] by pleading administrative interpretation."

The thirteen points were dead.

The following day Mitchell, unvanquished, commented, "It's becoming rather clear that what we wanted is not possible, literally, under the law. So my simple position is that the law should be changed."

The idea that new welfare laws were needed had become a central point in Mitchell's speeches which were taking him into nearly every section of the country. Since mid-summer Newburgh's chief executive had been traversing the United States like a candidate running for a national office. There were more than a few around Mitchell who began to suspect he was doing just that.

IN A REVEALING INTERVIEW in early 1962, Joe Mitchell told a feature writer for a Sunday newspaper magazine, "I know that my career as a city manager will end when I leave Newburgh. But I have dreams of other things. Having been born near Washington, I would hold in the highest honor the opportunity to be in Congress, the Senate or Cabinet."

Mitchell's words left no doubt of his interest in national office. But, contrary to what some of his critics have said, it is my impression that he did not hold such high ambitions prior to the national stir over the thirteen points.

"I knew we'd get favorable reaction," he told me in early summer 1961, "what we didn't expect was all the national publicity." And, although Mitchell was to become prominently identified with ultraconservatism, when I first met him in May 1961 he was careful not to label himself as a spokesman for any particular political belief.

I recall a conversation I had with him at the time in which we discussed the growing power of the Federal Government. Mitchell, though undoubtedly at heart a states' righter, expressed no opinion on the desirability of a strong centralized government. In fact during the course of his life, the City Manager's opinion appears to have wavered about the subject. In a later conversation in 1962 Mitchell revealed that during the period he worked for Uncle Sam he believed that the growth of a strong federal government was inevitable, if not desirable. "I was a bureaucrat and had bureaucratic ideas then," he said.

Two things happened to Joe Mitchell in response to the catalyst of national acclaim—his political ideas began to jell, and his personality began undergoing a subtle change. At first, Mitchell, aware of his modest status as a small-town city manager, appeared slightly ill at ease answering questions thrown at him by a squad of big city reporters. His confidence grew as he learned he could do as well against the inside curves thrown by the major league newsmen as he could against the slow ballers in the bush league.

Mitchell's attitude toward the press changed too. During the first few months of the controversy his door was always open to reporters, regardless of whether they were from friendly or hostile newspapers. Then, because perhaps he was stung by criticism and was growing wary, he stopped giving private interviews to newsmen he regarded as critical.

I recall that shortly after *The New York Times* published its first editorial on the thirteen points in which it referred to some of them as "dark-age rules," Mitchell confided to me that he had dissuaded McKneally from replying. "I told him we didn't want to take on *The New York Times*," he declared.

The remark was made early in July 1961. Yet by late summer Mitchell's confidence in his support had grown so that in a speech before the Rotary Club of the Bronx on September 26, he did not hesitate to refer to the *Times* as a member of "that fraternity of saboteurs of the nation, who will, if permitted, lead us down the fatal road of state socialism."[1]

As Mitchell became more cocksure, he abandoned all caution in his public remarks. He discovered what all modern demagogues learn—the more extreme his remarks became, the bigger play he received in the newspapers. Liberals became "the rapists of our society."[2] He espoused "thought control" and compared city newcomers to vegetables.

There is another weakness in most of our press which Mitchell learned to use to his advantage. That is, if a prominent person, as Mitchell became, says something sensational —even if false—it will be reported to the public without challenge. An attempt may be made the following day to print a comment by an authority on the other side of the issue, but often these authorities are reluctant or, because of their position, unable to become embroiled in controversy. The press pays no favorite to falsehood or truth, lest it be accused of the cardinal sin of editoralizing.

Thus, Mitchell was able to tell the women members of a Newburgh veterans' auxiliary that 20 to 30 per cent of the maternity cases at the city's only hospital were unmarried mothers and have it reported as gospel by the newspaper, despite the fact it would indicate that nearly one-third of the area infants were bastards. Several days later, no one paid much attention when a hospital official emphatically denied Mitchell's statistics.

[1] Other members of the "fraternity," Mitchell indicated, included *The Washington Post,* and *The Reporter* magazine, both of which published lengthy articles against the Newburgh program.

[2] From a speech given before the Queens Chapter, Young Americans for Freedom, September 18, 1961.

Some of Mitchell's statements may have appeared to the knowledgeable to be the products of a misinformed and biased mind, but they caught the headlines, as the City Manager intended, and they found a response in the masses.

"The roots of the welfare state go back to the doctrines of men like Sigmund Freud," he told those gathered at a Protestant communion breakfast. Freud asserted, Mitchell told his audience, "that the individual has no responsibility before God or man for his conduct." Since Clarence Darrow defended Leob and Leopold, he continued, "criminal lawyers and all the mushy rabble of do-gooders and bleeding hearts in society and politics have marched under the Freudian flag toward the omnipotent state of Karl Marx." The idea that an individual is a victim of his environment, he told me in a published interview later, "is opposed to all religious principles and has proven to be wrong."

From July 1961 to mid-January 1962 Mitchell made nearly fifty major out-of-town speeches to cities as far away as Houston, Texas and Milwaukee, Wisconsin. For a man who was unknown less than a year before, Mitchell had attained national recognition swiftly. Most of the speeches were before business and conservative groups such as the League of Conservative Voters, the Young Americans for Freedom, the Conservative Youth Group of New York City, the Economic Club of Detroit, and the Kiwanis Club of New York City.

But some were before GOP organizations ranging in size and importance from the Pennsylvania Council of Republican Women to the Wauwatosa (Wisconsin) Republican Club. In addition, the City Manager often appeared on radio and television in the cities he was visiting. By now, he had become a veteran TV performer, ac-

In March 1962 Mitchell made the most of his hero status among the conservative right. Here at the Hotel New Yorker in New York City, Vito P. Battista, Chairman of the United Taxpayer's Party, presents the "Taxpayer's Best Friend" award to Mitchell. Mrs. Mitchell looks on.

customed to having his impulsive viewpoint and fleshy figure broadcast over the national networks.

At home in Newburgh, his foes attacked his many out-of-town appearances. They said he wasn't devoting enough time to running the city, that he had political ambitions, and that he was using welfare as a means of personal gain. (Mitchell never revealed how much he was paid for his speaking appearances, but he signed a contract with a lecture agency which quoted his fee as $400 per appearance plus expenses. "It involves a lot of personal time," he told a reporter, "if I get any compensation I feel it's well earned.")

In a speech before the Delaware Valley Council, a body of industrialists and businessmen from the Philadelphia area, Mitchell gave his own reasons for accepting his busy speaking schedule:

> It was only after the gigantic reaction throughout the United States, and only after reading of the plight of similar cities, municipalities, counties and states did we realize how important the Newburgh story is to everyone. . . .
>
> I have accepted these speaking engagements in order to recite the details of the Newburgh story and to frankly encourage action in other parts of the nation, because we now feel after examining the situation in all its ramifications, that not only is state action needed, but action is needed on the national level to correct abuses to the taxpayers due to the ideologies, the philosophies, the theories and the laws of public welfare in the United States today, which, if unchecked, will without doubt, wreck the economy and social order of every territorial unit within the United States and its possessions.

And in a speech before the Newburgh Junior Chamber of Commerce, Mitchell contended: "It is not a political

issue in the normal sense. . . . This is primarily a question
of the liberal view as opposed to the conservative view."

Mitchell's speeches were always read from a text, copies
of which were distributed to the press in advance. He was
not an exciting speaker. His addresses were delivered in a
quiet monotone. There was little animation and no humor.
Nevertheless, they were enthusiastically received by audiences who shared his beliefs before he said a single word.
Before the few critical audiences to which he spoke, Mitchell appeared uneasy and belligerent.

His standard speech, given before non-Newburgh audiences, was twenty-four double-spaced, typewritten pages
long. It began with a quotation by Senator Barry Goldwater:

> My aim is not to pass laws, but to repeal them. It is not to
> inaugurate new programs, but to cancel old ones that do
> violence to the constitution, or that have failed in their pur-
> pose, or that impose on the people an unwarranted finan-
> cial burden. I will not attempt to discover where legislation
> is needed before I have first determined whether it is con-
> stitutionally permissible. . . .

For a man who had just inaugurated the most controversial new local program in the nation, in defiance of
state laws, it seems an odd choice of quotations.

Joseph Mitchell asked his audiences,

> Why was it that one small city of thirty-one thousand
> people . . . could start a ruckus which was felt around the
> world?
> How is it that the actions of a tiny four-man majority of
> a five-man council became the subject of editorials, car-
> toons, denouncements, praise and hundreds of newsprint
> columns and articles across the land and abroad? What

caused fifteen thousand people to write in and support us? What caused certain university schools of social service to oppose us? What caused public welfare associations to oppose us? . . .

What caused the Secretary of Health, Education, and Welfare to show such sudden interest in the "way we are just drifting along" in welfare? What caused the national press to parade into Newburgh with pad, pencil, TV camera and radio tape for three months in endless procession? What caused the investigation by the state Board of Social Welfare . . . into the operation of welfare in the city of Newburgh? What caused the New York State Attorney General to seek an injunction against us? What caused a New York Supreme Court judge to grant this injunction? What could a little city by the Hudson have done to have caused such a furor?

We challenged the welfare state and everything it stood for.

A brief statistical description of the city followed this barrage of questions. "The influx of migrant-type citizens in ten years, together with a total population loss of one thousand and a permanent resident-type[3] loss of 4,075 is an important indication of the seriousness of our social changes and their portent for the future."

Mitchell's version of the chronological sequence of events which led to adoption of the thirteen points came next, followed by a summary of the points and a statement of Mitchell's welfare philosophy.

Our position is that unless welfare considers the perspective of the community's total economic and social situation,

[3] Mitchell substituted the term "migrant-type" for Negro, and the term "permanent resident-type" for white, an interesting and revealing use of the language.

work on individual cases is futile and wasteful. No arm of government, anywhere, has the right to spend tax dollars with no tangible results for the community as a whole. . . .

The welfare program as it is presently constituted does not, in our estimation, go beyond the strict precepts and preconceived philosophies of social welfare as a sphere unto itself. It must, in our opinion, broaden its outlook, correlate itself to the total efforts of government, local, state and national. It is just as much a part of the total effort of government as police. It cannot and should not thrive in secrecy, nor should it be permitted to isolate its efforts. There is a crying need for reappraisal of the role of welfare in our society.

Mitchell's speech ended with his asking for legislation which would allow local welfare districts to rule themselves entirely, even though they were receiving state and federal funds.

Local policy control should rest with elected officials on the local level. In this manner the administration of public welfare at the local level will comprehend and reflect the wishes of the people of each area, be these wishes radical welfare, or conservative welfare.

The result will be a welfare program which the people want, not a welfare program which the bureaucrats think the people want. All of this is based on the assumption that most people want less government and more freedom. . . . Federal, state and local governments should back out of the welfare business. Welfare is not a proper government responsibility as it is now operated, and furthermore the facts have proved that the present theory and philosophy has failed. The social and economic results have been catastrophic. . . .

I propose that national plans be formulated to call a halt

to further welfare legislation, then to reduce its size and scope to an absolute minimum compatible with the proper roles of private charities, the churches and families.

I propose that aid to the truly needy be largely the responsibility of families, the churches and private charity agencies. . . . Do this and you will find that 90 per cent of all welfare cases will disappear overnight.

To audiences who regarded themselves overburdened by taxes which they felt were being used to support the shiftless, the irresponsible, and the incompetent, Mitchell's simple proposal brought a swelling response. The churches and private agencies themselves were not so enthusiastic. "The task is too large," I was told repeatedly by officials of religious and independent charitable organizations. Direct financial assistance by private charities has been on a very small scale since the 1930's when—faced with the inability of the independent agencies and the state governments to cope with widespread poverty—the Federal Government was forced to move into the field by default.

It is unrealistic to assume that if taxes were cut by the amount paid for public assistance, all the money would be donated to charity. To do so would mean that Americans would be donating $5½ billion, yearly (the amount in federal, state and local funds currently going to welfare recipients), or eleven times the amount they annually give to the United Fund.

Actually, although it is the social welfare program most commonly blamed for rising taxes, public assistance imposes a very light burden on the taxpayer. Federal, state, and local welfare payments combined comprise less than 1 per cent of the gross national product. The major portion of public assistance comes from federal funds. Nevertheless, this portion makes up only about 3 per cent of the national budget. Furthermore, putting the burden of public assistance on local charities means that those areas with the most poverty and highest rates of unemployment would also have the least resources to feed and clothe the needy.

It was ironic that Mitchell should be advocating the turning over of public assistance to local agencies. As he implied in his secret memo to the council, Newburgh could not operate its welfare department without outside help. The city, with its high percentage of low-income residents and inability to tax the wealthier home owners living just outside its borders, is an example of the need to spread the cost of welfare over a broader tax base. Its financial problems would have been impossible were it not that most of its welfare costs were paid by the state and federal governments.

Mitchell has sometimes been compared with the late Senator Joseph McCarthy. Like the former Appleton, Wisconsin judge who became the most conspicuous senator of his time, Mitchell suddenly rose from a public office in a small community to national prominence. Like McCarthy, who achieved considerable personal power by making his name synonymous with anti-communism, Mitchell seized a popular issue—welfare chiseling—and used it as a vehicle to launch himself into political orbit.

Paradoxically, while both men have been acclaimed for their political courage, the persons they attacked, however justifiably, represent a tiny slice of the voting public. Again like McCarthy, Mitchell is a right winger who used the speaker's platform to accuse the Federal Government of leading the country into communism. In a New York City speech he told a group of Young Americans for Freedom,

Collectivism is communism. Karl Marx, Friedrich Engels,

Joseph Stalin, and Nikolai Lenin, together with their successor, Nikita Khrushchev, all endorsed and employed the
principle of collectivism. . . . The collectivist principle is
part and parcel of the present United States grant-in-aid
system, the United States agricultural system, and, in fact,
much of the present United States federal pattern.

Having equated federal policies with communism, Mitchell
continued:

Are these men in positions of leadership in the Federal
Government in Washington, D.C. aware of the end result
of their policies? . . . Do they know that it [collectivism]
is the basis of government in the USSR? . . . Surely, they
know these things, yet, in face of this, . . . they keep repeating and inventing schemes to further the cause of collectivism.

It was to groups like the YAF, which had wholeheartedly
endorsed his welfare policy, that Mitchell most sounded as
though he had taken his line of reasoning from William
Buckley's ultra conservative journal *The National Review*
—and turned right.

He intimated to members of the Bergen County YAF
Chapter that welfare was being used as a communist tool
to destroy United States democracy:

Look about the metropolitan areas of the United States.
. . . Study the changes that have taken place. Study the
rise in crime rates. Study the rise in fire and sanitation in-
cidents, in disease; see the crowded housing. See the unemployment rate. Notice the change in social habits. . . .
Realize that a large percentage of the population is on relief—this does not include those on unemployment benefits
and social security payments. Notice that the United States
is spending one-third of its total budget to support a small
percentage of the population. [Although the last two sen-

tences contradicted each other, neither Mitchell, nor his audience of mostly college students, seemed aware of it.]

Notice that most of those on relief are made up in large part of those who are wrecking our cities.

What more could a communist ask?

Invariably, following his speeches before the YAF groups, the balding City Manager was applauded by his crew-cut listeners. The biggest tribute from the YAF was given in late August when some 200 members traveled by boat up the Hudson to present a plaque to their hero. Ironically, the excursion boat which carried the states' rights supporters was named the *Alexander Hamilton,* after the early American statesman who fought so vigorously for a strong federal government.

The Young Americans for Freedom arrived, in shirt sleeves and Bermuda shorts, at 2:15 on a warm, sunlit Saturday afternoon. Many looked too young to vote, but a few gray-haired "Young Americans" were scattered in the group. A police motorcycle escort and a dozen spectators greeted them at the dock. After milling around for several minutes they began a ragged march, three and four abreast, to City Hall, led by the motorcycles and a hatless young man carrying the Stars and Stripes.

The march had the appearance of a combined political convention demonstration and a college pep rally. Many carried signs with such slogans as: "Newburgh, Yes— Bureaucrats, No"; "YAF for Joe Mitchell"; "Down With the Welfare Chiselers"; and "Thirteen Points Heard Round the World." Some of the banners identified colleges or localities. One at the head of the parade read, "Hunter College YAF." Others said, "Queens County YAF," and "Yonkers YAF."

A bespectacled blonde girl wearing black Bermuda shorts and a checkered blouse led some of the marchers in a song to the tune of "Camptown Races":

> Welfare lines are five miles long,
> Do da. Do da.
> What can be done to correct this wrong?
> O, do da day.
> Down with the welfare state
> Before it's too late.
> YAFs for freedom think
> That Mitchell's great.

Others chanted: "We want Mitchell. We want Mitchell. We want Mitchell. We want Mitchell and his thirteen points."

At times along the route the marchers switched to a song in praise of Senator Goldwater to the music of "John Brown's Body": "We'll be back in '64 with Barry at the helm. Glory, glory hallelujah!"

Their route took them through the dilapidated buildings and empty stores in the Negro District bounding the waterfront. A few Negro men and women watched them bewilderedly from doorsteps and street corners. Drawn by the parade, a pack of about thirty Negro boys and girls happily walked alongside. Not until they reached City Hall where Mitchell and a crowd of nearly one hundred residents were waiting was there any applause for the group.

Joe Mitchell greeted his young supporters from a flag-bunted, second-floor balcony outside his office. His appearance was met with shouts and enthusiastic applause. Bareheaded in the sunlight, Mitchell looked down at the ring of mostly college-age men and women standing in the middle of the main street and read a brief speech.

Middletown (N.Y.) *Record*

Young Americans for Freedom march through Newburgh's Negro section on their way to City Hall.

It warned, "the future of this nation is perilled by the steady rise of federal bureaucracy, by the ever-perplexing and self-reversing decisions of the Supreme Court . . . [and] by the socialist theories, both economic and social, which have become accepted in all walks of life, particularly in the universities."

Mitchell's normally quiet voice, magnified by two loudspeakers, could be heard by patrons leaving a movie theater nearly two blocks away, as he asked: "Do we not have responsible legislators on the national level?"

A thunderous *No!* from his audience below interrupted the city manager's talk.

"Do we not have responsible department secretaries in Washington, D.C.?"

Again a roar of *No* answered him.

When he finished his speech, Mitchell went down into the street to receive a wooden plaque, about two feet long, mistakenly inscribed to James McDowell Mitchell. It was presented, the inscription said, "in recognition of [Mitchell's] courageous action for sound public welfare and his firm commitment to the principle of municipal responsibility."

After the ceremonies and the speeches were ended, the Young Americans for Freedom ambled back toward the dock in groups of two and three. There was no police escort and no singing. Most of the signs had been discarded. Some of the younger males were overheard telling crude jokes about life in the sticks.

At 4:15 P.M., two hours after their arrival, the group reboarded the *Alexander Hamilton*. Its members sailed for Manhattan, leaving Mitchell a misnomered plaque and something more meaningful—the memory of a crowd chanting his name. It would nourish any man with political desires.

Mitchell's political possibilities were already being considered by a group of former Young Republicans alienated from the party by what they considered its increasing liberal hue. They included William F. Buckley, Jr., publisher of the *National Review* and sometimes called the spiritual leader of the YAF; William A. Rusher, editor of the magazine; J. Daniel Mahoney, New York City lawyer and a member of the YAF advisory board; and Kieran O'Doherty, also a young New York City lawyer and a member of the board of directors of the Greatest New York Council of the YAF.

Mahoney and O'Doherty, together with two other Manhattan lawyers, Robert M. Saunders and Paul N. Cheney; an investment counsel, Richard R. Doll; and Paul Franklin, an investment analyst, had on July 4 formed the New York State Conservative Political Association which was to be the parent organization of the Conservative Party. During the summer and fall Mitchell met several times with members of the group in New York City. Politics, naturally, was the chief topic and the City Manager was sounded out on his availability to run against either Javits or Rockefeller in 1962.

Mitchell was made a definite offer of the senatorial nomination at a dinner on October 13 held in The Leash, a man's club restricted to dog breeders and trainers, located at 41 East 63rd Street in Manhattan. Albert F. Winslow, founder of the Citizens for Solvent Government, and the host at the dinner, points to the occasion as the founding of the Conservative Party.

Present besides Winslow and Mitchell were O'Doherty,

who was to become party chairman before running as its losing candidate for senator; Mahoney, who later took over the chairmanship from O'Doherty; Rusher; and Harry F. Weyher of New York City. At the request of Mitchell, William J. Simmons of Jackson, Mississippi, national administrator of the Citizens Councils of America, the co-ordinating body of southern white-supremacy organizations, was made a member of the party. Simmons, ranked as an extremist even by Mississippi standards, was to become better known as the chief strategist in the campaign to keep James Meredith out of the University of Mississippi.

According to Winslow, the white-supremacy leader played only a minor role in the discussions. He was, however, sympathetic to the conservative cause and expressed interest in forming a Conservative Party in the South.

But for the present, the immediate aim of the Mahoney-O'Doherty-Rusher coterie was to find candidates who could cut the expected margin of victory by Rockefeller and Javits in 1962. In accomplishing this, the young GOP dissenters hoped to forge a lever with which to move the state party further to the right.[4]

With the consent of the others, O'Doherty offered the

[4] As of this writing, the Conservatives have achieved only part of their aims. Their candidate for governor, David H. Jaquith, polled 118,768 votes in the 1962 elections, cutting Rockefeller's victory margin to 518,218, more than 55,000 short of his 1958 plurality. Furthermore, in attracting more than the required 50,000 votes, the party was assured of a place on future tickets.

On the other hand, O'Doherty, who won only 83,585 votes out of a total of more than 5½ million, did little harm to Javits, who gained a plurality of nearly one million, highest on the state ticket. In 1964 the only state-wide Conservative candidate, Henry Paolucci, a professor of history and political science at Iona College, received only 2.5 per cent of the vote when he ran for the senate against Kenneth Keating and Robert Kennedy.

In Washington, D.C., on July 15, 1961, now national front-page news, Mitchell outlines his 13-point program to reporters.

senatorial nomination to Mitchell. Before the City Manager could reply, Mahoney broke in to point out to Mitchell that he had hardly any chance of winning. Winslow says that Mitchell was irritated by Mahoney's statement and testily refused the offer, stating he was not interested in anything "preordained to failure."

How definite was Mitchell's refusal? He, himself, claims he never accepted any of the Conservative Party's bids, which is undoubtedly true. Nevertheless, events in the following month indicate the door was not quite shut.

Before describing the November events, it is an interesting sidelight to note that as early as midsummer Mitchell was responsible for a battle between the right and left wings of the Republican party.

Called to Washington, D.C. on July 15—the day the thirteen points went into effect—to speak before a conference sponsored by the conservative magazine, *Human Events,* he was invited to return to the capital the following week to attend a breakfast honoring newly-elected Texas Republican Senator John H. Tower, and to confer with Senator Barry Goldwater.

Senator Goldwater had the previous week sent Mitchell a telegram in which he called the welfare plan "as refreshing as breathing the clean air of my native Arizona."

The announcement of the conference between the two men caused some members of the press to suggest that Goldwater might be making a political issue out of the welfare battle in order to embarrass the leader of the liberal wing of the Republican party, Governor Rockefeller, in his home territory.

The Republican *New York Herald Tribune,* a Rockefeller supporter, despite being an early backer of the Newburgh code, editorialized:

Neither Sen. Barry Goldwater nor Newburgh City Manager Joseph Mitchell is likely to profit from the public association created by their ill-conceived interview in Washington.

. . . For Sen. Goldwater to serve up Newburgh as Exhibit A in his anti-welfare campaign, to attempt to make an issue of it in his supposed contest with Gov. Rockefeller is shabby. Mr. Mitchell is obviously the dupe of his own inexperience in national politics.

In moral and human terms, the Newburgh plan rightfully enlisted a considerable degree of support. In terms of political jockeying, it runs the risk of being totally discredited.

The offices of Senators Goldwater and Tower denied that any indirect attack on Rockefeller was intended in the scheduling of the meetings. "My meeting with Mr. Mitchell was simply for the purpose of exchanging views with a city official whose courage I admire," Senator Goldwater stated to the press in Washington following a twenty-minute private talk with Newburgh's chief executive.

His telegram endorsing the city's program, he said, was

dictated solely by my personal feelings about a problem which is victimizing honest American taxpayers who are being called upon to support and pay for dishonesty.

I wrote Mr. Mitchell as one citizen to another and as a person who once served as a city councilman and who has some knowledge of the problem with which he is confronted. . . . There's nothing political in this.

The Senator's denials failed to convince most political observers.

But if Senator Goldwater had intended to make political hay out of his association with Mitchell, he must have later regretted he had sown the crop. As the *Herald Tribune* had anticipated, the association proved to be embarrassing to the Arizona conservative.

By an ironic coincidence, the hope of the Conservative Party to run Mitchell against Javits was made public during a convention at which the City Manager and Goldwater appeared together as guest speakers. The knowledge that he was then chairman of the Republican Senatorial Campaign Committee must have made the disclosure doubly embarrassing for the Phoenix legislator. The story which exposed the wishes of the incipient third party appeared in the Long Island newspaper, *Newsday*, on November 14—harvest time. It was picked up by the Associated Press and carried nationally.

The City Manager and the Senator at the time were attending the annual conference of the Pennsylvania Council of Republican Women being held in Harrisburg. Mitchell was caught by surprise.

"I like my job in Newburgh. I'm very happy there," he told reporters who cornered him in Harrisburg as fast as they could say "political candidate." The splinter political group advocated a viewpoint close to his own, he acknowledged, "but I'm not interested in running for the Senate at this time." It was as much, or as little, as any candidate could be expected to say under such circumstances. Mitchell continued, "Anyone who has been in government all his life, as I have, would naturally look upon elected office as the highest honor possible. I would consider it a great honor. But I'm happy as city manager."

Back in Newburgh a reporter asked McKneally what he thought of the latest development. "You can report me, for the first time, as having no comment," he snapped.

McKneally found his voice five days later, after *Newsday* on November 17 disclosed that Mitchell would be one of

the two[5] keynote speakers at the Conservatives' kickoff
rally in a Garden City hotel on November 30. The purpose
of the rally, the newspaper said, was to test public reaction
to formation of the splinter party and to the two men it
would like to run for governor and senator. On November
20 McKneally contacted me at the newspaper office to say
that two days before he had telephoned Joe Mitchell in
Detroit, where the City Manager was making a speech.
McKneally said he thought he had convinced Mitchell that
it would not be to his advantage to make the scheduled
Garden City address. "The address would be tantamount to
throwing his hat in the ring," the Republican councilman
observed in a tone that indicated his annoyance with the
City Manager.

When I asked what would happen if Mitchell went ahead
with his planned speech, McKneally replied, "I think the
inference is there." The statement left little doubt that
McKneally would attempt to dump Mitchell if he disobeyed
his wishes in the matter.

"Joe's a little too naive for his own good," McKneally
observed. "It may be that the Conservatives have persuaded
him to run against the judgement of his city directors."

Since late summer Councilmen McIntyre and Green had
been critical of the amount of time Mitchell was spending
outside of Newburgh on his speaking trips. The City Manager's interest in a political office now prompted McKneally
to join them. "I believe that Mitchell's speaking engagements have accomplished their purpose in selling the need

---

[5] The other scheduled speaker was the Conservatives' then-
reported candidate for governor, Godfrey Schmidt, a New York City
lawyer who served as counsel to a group of Teamster Union members who rebelled against the union's domination by James R. Hoffa.
Schmidt later bowed out of the running.

for welfare reforms across the country," McKneally told
me. "Further speaking engagements are unnecessary and
the time has come for all of us to devote full time and attention to the affairs of Newburgh."

It was obvious that McKneally's public statement was intended as a warning to Mitchell in case the Conservatives
should try to persuade him to honor his commitment to
address their rally. But why was McKneally so strongly
opposed to Mitchell's third party candidacy? Part of the
reason was disclosed in the plumber-politician's statement.

"Since I was primarily responsible for bringing Mitchell
to Newburgh, I should be the first to recognize his derelic-
tion," McKneally declared. "I'm a conservative, but I'm a
Republican first and these people are trying to injure the
Republican party."

Even stronger than McKneally's loyalty to the GOP, is
his loyalty to his bachelor brother, Martin. The fact that
Martin McKneally would like the Republican nomination
for congressman was an open secret in Orange County political circles. But the chances of the former National
Commander of the American Legion getting the party's
nomination would be considerably lessened if the man
George McKneally brought to New York tried to unseat an
incumbent Republican. The Newburgh Councilman was
made acutely aware of that fact by top state GOP officials.

The day after McKneally's thinly-veiled warning was
published in the Newburgh *Evening News,* Mitchell announced that he had canceled his November 30 address. He
also declared he had "flatly disassociated [himself] in any
manner with that conservative movement." His reason, he
said, was because "it would reflect on [his] status as a
Republican."

"If I were to associate myself with these conservatives, I

would have to divorce myself from the Republican party and I don't want to do that ever. Being a staunch Republican, I have no wish to embarrass the party." Mitchell's newfound concern for the Grand Old Party was amusing to anyone who had been reading his speeches before conservative-minded organizations. In one such speech Mitchell told the Queens Chapter of the YAF:

> I have heard from a reliable source that the conservative and YAF movement is doomed because they will argue amongst themselves and defeat their purpose. Don't let this happen, for if you do, you will play into the hands of the liberals, OF BOTH POLITICAL PARTIES[6] who are counting on this to destroy your movement, so that the radicals, liberals, socialists and leftists may continue their drive towards state socialism and the destruction of the Republic as we have known it.

Contrary to all established codes of proper conduct for a non-partisan city manager, Mitchell in August released a public statement endorsing the young Conservative candidate Edward L. Nash in his bid to dislodge a highly-respected Republican, Stanley Isaacs, from his seat on the New York City Council. Mr. Nash lost his bid in the primaries by 908 votes, a fact which Newburgh's chief administrator commented on in his Queens YAF speech:

> I shall not dwell on the honesty or dishonesty of the machine opposing Mr. Nash, but on the fact that Ed Nash had made a significant dent in the hard shell of liberal Republicans in New York City. He has established himself and the cause of conservativism in the hearts and minds of the thinking, responsible, ethical public. I have no doubt that the next time Ed Nash runs . . . he will win with an overwhelming majority.

[6] The capitalization is Mitchell's, written in his prepared text.

Strange words for a "staunch Republican."

A few hours after Mitchell canceled his scheduled speech the Conservative forum was also cancelled. Edward Werner, owner of *The Long Island Review,* a conservative weekly which was sponsoring the forum, claimed "Republican bosses" put pressure on Mitchell not to go ahead with his planned address. "Reports reaching us are that the Nassau bosses immediately moved through the Albany bosses to reach the Newburgh bosses, and Mr. Mitchell was informed that the Liberal Republicans had removed freedom of speech as one of his constitutional rights," said Mr. Werner, obviously a man who disliked bosses.

In Newburgh, the following day Mitchell commented "This [Mr. Werner's statement] is exactly why I canceled the engagement. This group will not do the cause of Republicanism any good whatsoever."

Mitchell's remarks made it plain that his severance with the Conservatives as a separate political party was complete.

There is no evidence that Mitchell ever made a wholehearted commitment to become a Conservative candidate. He realized, without Mahoney's telling him, that despite all his popular backing, his chances of unseating a respected incumbent senator by running on a third party ticket supported by a hastily-constructed, amateurish political machine were about equivalent to his becoming heavyweight boxing champion.

Furthermore, Mitchell was not a wealthy man who could afford to give up his position as well as possible future opportunities in the city manager field in order to be used as a pawn to strengthen the position of conservatives in the Republican party. Yet, there are few men who ever get the chance to become a candidate for a major national office. Such a man inevitably receives a respectable share of attention in the press and the warming praise of party well-wishers—two things Mitchell found irresistible. Then too, the welfare issue which launched the City Manager into national prominence was at the apex of its flight. Soon, it seemed then, it would be on its downward course toward obscurity and with it the name of Joseph McDowell Mitchell. There was very little likelihood that he would ever again have an opportunity to see his name so high on the ballot.

These thoughts must have crossed Mitchell's mind many times that fall as he teetered on the edge of the political diving board, wondering if it was worthwhile plunging into the cold campaign waters. Only Mitchell knows if he had fully made up his mind before he was ordered away from the pool.

What kind of a platform Mitchell would have campaigned on had he become a candidate for a national office can be guessed from a speech he delivered in Troy, New York, on November 12, 1963, following his resignation as city manager. In it he opposed nearly every major piece of social or economic legislation enacted by the Federal Government in this century. Among the federal programs and organizations he advocated eliminating were urban renewal, the United States Employment Service (Mitchell asserted that it deprives private employment agencies of fees), farm subsidies, welfare aid, and the Peace Corps.

One Faulknerian sentence near the end of the speech summarizes its message:

In our individual rush to get grants-in-aid for our locality, in our emotional fervor to feed, clothe, and house the population of the world indefinitely and forever, in our willingness to subsidize every citizen who comes along, in our misguided compassion over welfare and medicare, in our futile designs to reform foreign lands to our image—or to reform our aid to their image—in our foolhardy application of unproved economic theories to national spending, taxation and debt, in our dangerous use of federal troops against our own people, in our willingness to let the Supreme Court sink to political involvement, use psychology and sociology as authority, or substitute its decisions for laws, in our misuse of education for sociological ends, in our readiness to compete with the natural forces of free enterprise by using public funds in housing, employment and other fields, in reversing the ratio of state and local funds to federal spending, in our exoneration of elected representatives for using the Congress as an olympic stadium of competition in new government spending and control devices, in our docile acceptance of endless forms of backbreaking taxation and unbridled spending for every conceivable purpose, in the folly of suppressing God so as to be "fair" to agnostic freaks, and in many, many other ways, we are remolding our society, our economic system, and our form of government to reconstitute all of the evils our forefathers gave their lives to eliminate.

In his speech, which Mitchell had intended for delivery at college campuses on the West Coast, he delineated a political philosophy based largely on a world of his own making and a shallow knowledge of the Constitution. "Life is far simpler today than in the past," he maintained. The only things making life complex, according to Mitchell, are the studies and theories of the economists, the sociologists, psychologists, and government officials.

It was the intent of the Constitution that the federal government handle only those matters affecting the state which were of an inter-state basis, i.e., matters requiring coordination or uniformity, such as currency, national defense, patents, and other such matters.

Nowhere in the Constitution is it indicated that the President is to be any more than the chief administrative officer, such as a county executive, responsible for carrying out the will of the people as expressed through Congress. By the same token, Congress was to pass only those laws which pertained to the necessary coordination of states affairs.

The Supreme Court is an appeal body with no power to enforce its decisions, but with the primary role of settling disputes between the states, or ruling on matters beyond the jurisdiction of individual states.

[Nowhere in the Constitution] is any authority for the federal government to operate programs for medicare, for farm subsidization, for welfare, for foreign aid, for public housing, or for any number of programs, such as the Peace Corps, which have been creeping up on us within the past thirty years.

As Mitchell had indicated previously, he took a dim view of the current civil rights battle waged by Negroes. "One of the greatest tragedies of our times is the shameless exploitation of the Negro masses by white politicians and ambitious Negro rights leaders," he wrote in his prepared speech. "I and many Americans of all races feel that today's 'racial crisis' is synthetic, that in actuality the overwhelming majority of Negroes are no more dissatisfied with their lot than others in like circumstances are with theirs."

Mitchell, who had administered the public policies of a city of 31,000 with marked lack of success, freely gave his views on the United Nations and foreign affairs. He maintained:

The world needs a public forum, but the world doesn't

need nor can it afford world government. Nationalism, a
term which has taken on a derogatory connotation these
days, is actually what makes a country great.

Having said this, Mitchell, a few sentences later, illogi-
cally launched an attack on African nationalism.

We are urged by our State Department and our UN am-
bassador to lend our support to "freeing" the African nations. There is considerable doubt that the African people
understand, are ready for, or want freedom as we know it.
While many feel that colonialism is a perfectly proper way
of life, even if it isn't, no amount of United States aid over
the next three decades will bring about enough education,
industry, or facilities to permit the operation of these nations as free capitalist countries according to American
standards. Once benevolent colonialism is eliminated from
Africa, the door is opened to socialism, or dictatorships,
such as Algeria.

Mitchell's remarks indicated he would include the South
African Republic and Portuguese Angola as examples of
African "benevolent colonialism." "Both were made sub-
ject to arms embargoes, and both on the theory that racial
discrimination and colonialism threaten international peace.
The exact reverse is probably nearer the truth."

Only a relatively small portion of the speech dealt directly with public welfare. As would be expected, Mitchell
expressed no sympathy for those on the dole. Welfare recipients, without qualification, were to him "people whose
morality has failed them." The welfare program "has accomplished nothing except to cost you money, enlarge
slums, make relief a way of life, and expand the bureaucracy."

Being forced to cancel his Garden City speech was only

the first of two setbacks Mitchell received in November 1961. Like the first, the other was a reaction to his political activities.

Point seven of the ten-point Code of Ethics of the International City Managers' Association declares, in part, that a city manager "recognizes that the chief function of the local government at all times is to serve the best interests of all the people on a nonpartisan basis." On November 26 Mitchell was found guilty of violating that point by the ICMA executive committee at the organization's convention in Miami Beach. As a result, he was censured by the committee.

The City Manager's reaction was, as in previous similar situations, belligerent. "Apparently the ICMA would rather see a guy fired than have him defend himself," he snapped. He insisted that the association's action had nothing to do with his political stand.

> It's their way of saying they are against our welfare reforms. . . . It's a question of the net effect on the social welfare association. All our opponents can now say, "here's a city manager that is discredited by his own association, hence everything he has done is discredited . . ."
>
> They have taken the one instance in fifty years of city management which showed the true value of the council-manager plan and they perverted it.

Mitchell was never reluctant to hand out self-praise when he felt it was merited.

Mitchell's difficulties with the ICMA began even before he came to Newburgh. In 1959 the executive board met to consider a charge that he had taken part in a factional Republican fight while he was manager of Marple Township. The charge was vague, however, and nothing ever came of the meeting. Two years later, an ICMA official was to regret the board's lack of action. "The case warranted further investigation," he admitted. "We should have looked into it more than we did."

The association officials again began casting a critical eye at Mitchell in mid-1961 after he told the press he was a conservative Republican and a supporter of Barry Goldwater. At about the same time reporters began badgering ICMA officials in Chicago about their impressions of the organization's most prominent member. In July a *Middletown Record* reporter wrote that Robert Brenton, ICMA assistant director, told him Joe had given the profession a "black eye" by his political statements.

Early in August, Tracy Lucas of *The Baltimore Sun* telephoned Orin F. Nolting, executive director of the association, asking him if the ICMA sanctioned Mitchell's activities, and its opinion of the controversial welfare code. Nolting's reply by letter began a series of communications between Mitchell and association officials which reflected the growing cleavage between them. In his letter to Lucas, Nolting declared:

> I do feel that many of the changes which have been proposed and apparently approved in Newburgh are not in accord with sound public welfare administration.
> *The New York Times* for Aug. 4 carried a UPI story quoting City Manager Mitchell as saying he would use "thought control" on social workers employed by the city. This implies a kind of control that is not at all typical of city managers and is not in accord with good personnel practice.

Nolting sent a copy of his reply to Mitchell, and a few days later dispatched a note, which stated, in part:

> You have centered nation-wide attention on the welfare problem. It seems that many people, however, disagree

with the approach you have taken to this matter because it
seems some of the items in your welfare code adopted by
the Council are contrary to national and state law and
policy.

One thing of concern to me are the press reports which
quote you as saying that you are a Republican, indicating
perhaps that you have taken a partisan approach to the
problem. If this is true, then you may be in conflict with
the ICMA Code of Ethics.

If you have any comments in defense of this stand, assuming this partisan approach is correct, I shall be glad if
you would write me.

Mitchell wrote back on the day he received the copy of
the Nolting-Lucas letter:

I am somewhat disappointed in your reply to Tracy
Lucas. . . . The underlying principles of our efforts here
. . . are towards the improvement of the social and economic outlook of this city.

These efforts are therefore in full accord with the principles of sound public management. Welfare per se is but a
part of these efforts, and it shall be proven in court that 12
of these 13 points are lawful and could have been used by
any welfare commissioner in the state.

As to "thought control"—this, frankly, was taken out of
context by the wire services and I feel that anyone who
reads the article in detail will realize that our aim here is to
obtain new people, whose thoughts are aligned with the
good of the community as a whole, and who have a perspective philosophy in dealing with social matters.

It appears to me, regretfully, that the impression of your
letter, while, no doubt, perfectly well intended, will be to
such writers as Lucas, an indication that the ICMA is not in
support of Newburgh's position, and some doubt is cast by
the letter as to my professional standing.

I respectfully suggest that if there is any doubt in your

mind as executive director, and if there is any doubt in the
minds of the association, that rather than make further public statements of this kind, they delegate a representative to
come to this city and to examine in detail the entire situation.

The City Manager's reply was mailed before he received
Nolting's note. On receiving it, he dispatched a second letter. In it he defended his announcement that he was a Republican.

> I am a Republican and have registered Republican,
> where such registration would not cast unfavorable light on
> my duties.
> I assume that a manager is permitted to register accord-
> ing to his choice of political faith under the American sys-
> tem. I have never, however, employed partisan politics in ,
> my job. . . .

He repeated his invitation to Nolting to visit the city. The
ICMA head responded cordially to Mitchell's two letters
with one of his own. In it he commented:

> With regard to the welfare policies adopted by the City
> Council of Newburgh, I think it is a matter for the City
> Council to decide whether or not they are good policies for
> Newburgh. Certainly it is not for us to say what policies the
> City Council of any given city should adopt with regard to
> local services.
> I must say, however, that there has been some feeling on
> the part of managers in different parts of the country that
> the publicity which the City of Newburgh is receiving is
> harmful to the manager profession.
> P.S. Thanks also for your letter of Aug. 11 explaining the
> situation with regard to partisan politics. I am glad you are
> personally avoiding this approach and I am glad to have
> your statement.

There is no evidence of any more letters between Nolting and Mitchell. However, in a communication dated October 6, 1961, Raymond M. Urquhart, president of the City Managers' Association of New York State, who had earlier visited Newburgh to talk with Mitchell, wrote him:

> I met a few days ago with the vice president and secretary-treasurer of the City Mangers' Association of New York State in Rochester. We discussed, at this informal session . . . your problems, widely publicized in various news media, and concluded that perhaps much of the adverse publicity your community has received is as distressing to you as it has been to most, if not all, your colleagues in the city manager profession.
>
> With this thought in mind, it was decided that I should contact you to offer our assistance to bring an end to the unfortunate publicity directed toward your city and, I might add, you as city manager.

Mitchell's reply to Urquhart indicates the City Manager did not take the same gloomy view toward the publicity he was receiving:

> I appreciate the desire of the association to assist me and the City Council; I must, however, point out that, though controversial, the publicity we have received has not been adverse, either to me or the city.
>
> . . . It is my duty, as mandated by my City Council, to continue our drive with the objective that the state laws and the federal laws may be changed to grant each city the power of home rule. . . .

Mitchell brazenly suggested that if the New York State Managers' Association take any action, it endorse his proposed legislative changes to end state and federal control over local welfare programs. (The suggestion was not fol-

lowed by the state chapter. It would adopt only one action
—endorsement of Mitchell's later censure by the parent
body.)

The City Manager received one more letter from an
ICMA official. On October 9 R. H. van Dewsen, member of
the ICMA board of directors from Pennsylvania, wrote asking three questions, as he put it, to better inform himself before the November meeting of the board:

> 1. I have read . . . there has been no substantial basis
> for your allegation of welfare "chiselling" and that you did
> not, when pressed, really intend to put your program of wel-
> fare reforms into effect. Would you care to comment . . . ?
>
> 2. I have been questioned regarding the number of
> speaking engagements which you have accepted outside
> the city. Would you care to indicate why you have felt the
> need to advance Newburgh's views in other quarters rather
> than refer these outside speaking engagements to politically-
> elected representatives of the people of Newburgh?
>
> 3. Do you feel that you should continue to accept out-
> side speaking engagements and/or write articles for publi-
> cation advancing the Newburgh welfare concept?
>
> Your comments regarding these questions would be ap-
> preciated. I am most anxious to learn your personal views
> regarding the charges and counter charges surrounding the
> Newburgh welfare controversy.

Mitchell's answer, when he received the letter the following day, was brief and resentful:

> I regret very much the action which seems to be implied
> by your letter of Oct. 9. In view of the inference in this
> letter, I am referring it to my corporation counsel, Mr. Law-
> rence Herbst, who will represent me in all matters pertain-
> ing to my membership in the ICMA.

As this last note indicates, Mitchell was well aware that his political and other activities during the last months were endangering his membership in the ICMA. Yet on November 1 in a seemingly defiant gesture toward the association, he told a joint dinner meeting of the Women's Republican Club of Newburgh and the City Republican Committee that he would resign unless Doulin and McIntyre were not reelected in the elections to be held six days later. (The other two Republicans on the council, McKneally and Green, were not up for reelection until 1963.) Said the "nonpartisan" City Manager:

> I feel if this election fails to return the two councilmen to public office then it will be a repudiation of everything we have done and a warning to do no more.
>
> My effectiveness as city manager hinges on the wishes of the people as expressed in their choice of candidates on November 7. I therefore, offer my resignation as of December 31, if these two men are not reelected, and I challenge the mayor of Newburgh, William D. Ryan, to show the courage of his convictions by submitting his resignation on that date should his candidates not be elected.

It was on the basis of these remarks that the ICMA executive committee voted to censure Mitchell for "partisan political activity." The censure, itself, carried no penalty. Mitchell was permitted to maintain his membership in the association, which he did. In Newburgh the censure action not only failed to weaken his support among the public and the council majority, it intensified the impression being created that Joe was a fearless public official persecuted for his attempts to reform welfare evils.

"This outrageous interference into local affairs will not be tolerated by this City Council," McKneally thundered in a blistering telegram to the ICMA officials.

Nevertheless, the censure gravely hurt Mitchell's chances of becoming city manager in a bigger city at a higher salary. Even so, no one, certainly not Mitchell, could imagine that in slightly more than a year a scandal would occur which would seemingly bar him forever from public office, and which would bring upon him even sterner action by the Managers' Association.

ELEVEN · A CHARGE OF BRIBERY

IN THE HALF-DECADE beginning in 1957, when Joe Mitchell first set sail in the perilous water of municipal management, his course, as noted earlier, was beset by storms. Twice he had resigned from public posts under fire. He had been censured by the ICMA. Although in the beginning of his welfare program he had received popular support from the masses and the large circulation newspapers and magazines which attract their readership, such influential publications as *The New York Times* had been outspokenly critical. In January 1962 a special NBC "White Paper" entitled, "The Battle of Newburgh," devoted an hour of prime Sunday night time to picturing Mitchell as a power-seeking demagogue abusing the needy for his political aims.

Mitchell doggedly weathered all the storms. But in 1962 his popularity began to ebb. The welfare program had been declared illegal by the courts, despite the contentions of the city administration that it was acting within the law. Although the City Manager claimed he had successfully substituted psychological warfare for the invalid thirteen points, welfare costs continued to rise.

"Old men and wise men have set up laws and systems. They work at it all year, year after year, and then a young fellow comes along and tears them all down, and starts something new. This can get pretty close to rabble-rousing," a disillusioned elderly businessman told an out-of-town reporter.

"I was for him at the start because I thought there were a lot of chiselers getting relief," another resident declared thoughtfully. "But now I'm not convinced this was so. He talks about cleaning up slums but I don't think he has done it."

Mitchell might contend in his out-of-town speeches that the waterfront slums "have been visibly cleaned up,"[1] but as many Newburgh residents were aware, the fact was that blight continued to spread block by block westward from the Hudson. Four years after the welfare program was announced, few of the waterfront merchants who had been there in 1961 remained in the area. The city's only department store had moved to a new location outside of town.

One of the city's largest industries, a textile mill employing about two hundred and fifty, closed its doors permanently a week before Christmas 1962. Controversy over Mitchell and his programs continued to split the community into two warring camps. "You don't discuss welfare any more unless you know the person well," said the wife of a Newburgh attorney. "We've lost some of our best friends because of our disagreement with Mr. Mitchell's policies. There are some people who are fundamentally destructive, who radiate all the wrong things. Mitchell is one of them. He sows dissension and unhappiness."

"We are a torn, bitter and divided community with neighbor against neighbor and businessmen afraid of a loss of business if they speak," a young local lawyer told the council at one of its meetings.

[1] From an address before the Ohio-Indiana Council of Republican Women, October 6, 1961.

Even such strong supporters of Mitchell as Councilman Doulin began to remark: "I wish I had never heard of welfare." Residents of the city feared that outsiders thought most of the community consisted of slums and relief recipients. A native of Newburgh told me that when he went out-of-state he told people he was from the neighboring village of Cornwall. "I'm ashamed to tell them I live in Newburgh," he admitted.

Many of the businessmen and other leaders of the community who had supported Mitchell began to realize what Little Rock, Arkansas discovered half a decade earlier: Industry is reluctant to move into a community stirred by controversy. And Newburgh desperately needed new industry. As Mayor Ryan observed,

> I don't think people around here realized just how black a name their home town was getting until they saw the NBC "White Paper" on Newburgh. Up to then they'd been reading chiefly the local paper, which was all for Mitchell. But when they saw that program, with welfare recipients crying on the screen and found out that 15,000,000 other Americans saw it too, then I think they began wondering whether the whole thing was worth it.

Some of the Republican councilmen were wondering that too. Green and McIntyre demanded that Mitchell curtail the number of his speech-making trips and attend to business in the city. They were annoyed too that the welfare issue had increased city administrative costs. Just answering the fifteen thousand letters which came into Mitchell's office cost some $600 in postage, plus the hiring of an extra secretary. (In the city's books, however, she was listed as an employee of the city engineer's office. To be fair, she did perform a considerable share of work in the office after the welfare

issue died down.) In addition, there was the cost of mimeo-
graphing copies of Mitchell's speeches which were distributed by the handful to the press and radio and to visitors and
well-wishers.

However disillusioned Green and McIntyre may have
been with their City Manager, their feelings in late November 1962 were not strong enough to stop them from voting
with Doulin and McKneally to raise Mitchell's salary $1,550
to $15,700 annually. Two weeks later they learned that the
man they had recently rewarded was being accused of solic-
iting $20,000 for himself as a bribe. It was the beginning
of a five-month period Mitchell was to call "my ordeal."

Mitchell's ordeal had its sudden beginning on December
7, 1962. The main local story in *The Evening News* was
that the owners of the Stroock textile mill, which once employed more than five hundred, had declined offers by community financial interests which would keep it open. Two
days of rain had given way to snow flurries and the weather-
man predicted heavy snowfall in the afternoon.

In New York City the chief topic was whether the International Typographers Union would carry out a threatened
strike of some of the city's newspapers scheduled for two the
following morning.

The City Manager's schedule for the day was light. The
chief item on his calendar was a hearing on a rezoning matter at four that afternoon. Twin brothers from Monticello,
about sixty miles northwest, wanted to have eleven and a
half acres of property they owned in the city rezoned so they
could build apartments on it. It was routine city business
which had merited passing mention in the newspaper the
day before.

At noon Mitchell went to lunch at Lugi's, an Italian restaurant four doors from McKneally's plumbing establish-

ment on Broadway, the city's main street, and seven blocks from City Hall. McKneally joined Mitchell at the bar several minutes later and the two went into the dining room where they shared a table. After lunching, the Councilman returned to his office. It was starting to snow.

Mitchell remained and talked to friends. At about 1:30 P.M. he received a telephone call. He received a second call ten minutes later. Both were from the Manhattan hotel room of a Lawrence J. DeMasi, Jr., a New Jersey real estate promoter whom Mitchell had referred to the Monticello brothers as the middle-man in their rezoning efforts.

After the second call, Mitchell remained in Lugi's drinking Scotch and sodas until 3:30 P.M. when he returned to his office, glanced at the agenda, and said a few words to Mrs. Hollis Taylor, his secretary.

But he was restless. After telling Mrs. Taylor he would be a little late for the rezoning hearing, he got into his convertible and drove gingerly—the streets were snow-covered now—back to Lugi's where he had another drink at the bar before walking to McKneally's office. It was 4:30 P.M. Although the meeting was scheduled for four, the next forty-five minutes were spent in the plumbing establishment.

Meanwhile, at City Hall, Joseph P. Fogarty, a Newburgh lawyer representing the Monticello brothers, Joseph and Stephen Wahrhaftig, waited for the hearing to begin. Waiting with him were Mayor Ryan and Corporation Counsel Herbst. At 4:45 P.M. Ryan left, just before the arrival of Councilman Doulin. Shortly after 5 P.M., Mitchell, McKneally, and Councilman Green arrived. Mitchell went into his office and returned a few minutes later to announce that the meeting would be delayed. He then left City Hall and returned to Lugi's where he was to meet DeMasi. The chubby real estate agent, an acquaintance of the City Manager's for a year and a half, was to figure prominently in Mitchell's life during the coming five months.

Mitchell stayed at the restaurant until 6:15 P.M. Upon his return to City Hall he was arrested by detectives from New York City District Attorney Frank S. Hogan's office. The charges against him, the detectives informed the City Manager, were accepting a bribe as a public officer and conspiracy to take a bribe to rezone the Wahrhaftig property.

Mitchell was understandably surprised to learn that a few minutes after he had last talked to DeMasi in the early afternoon the real estate agent had been arrested. In his possession was $20,000 in marked bills—a sum given to him minutes before by the Wahrhaftigs. The brothers claimed it was a bribe, intended for Mitchell, to rezone the property.

As dozens of movie stars and top political figures have discovered, fame is a drawback when one is accused of wrongdoing. Mitchell, who had built a false reputation as a warrior against minor chiselers, in a quick turnabout, was now accused of doing some major chiseling himself. What was supposed to be a routine rezoning hearing unexpectedly blossomed into a front page story in the next morning's newspapers.

Although the City Manager must have been jolted by his arrest, he never lost his composure—an aspect of Mitchell's makeup which served him during his trial. He acted with the gracious courtesy of a polished public servant showing important visitors his municipal domain as he allowed the detectives to search his desk and pointed out the location of office typewriters so they could take type impressions as evidence.

After making several telephone calls to obtain legal advice, Mitchell was driven to New York City. On his arrival, he was questioned briefly by Assistant District Attorney

Outside District Attorney Frank Hogan's Manhattan office, Mitchell tells reporters that he is innocent of the bribery charges.

Karl Grebow, a quiet-voiced methodical questioner with a benign manner and a pleasant face. Afterward, the City Manager was booked, fingerprinted, and photographed, just like any Newburgh welfare client.

Said Mitchell to reporters, "They've got the wrong man. I've never done anything wrong in my life."

Six days later a Manhattan grand jury returned an indictment against the City Manager and DeMasi, charging them with three felonies and a misdemeanor, all stemming from the alleged attempt to extort a bribe from the Wahrhaftigs. Faced with a maximum prison sentence of thirty years, they pleaded not guilty.

The reaction of Mitchell supporters to his arrest, once the shock of the announcement was over, was that the City Manager had been framed by "liberals and do-gooders" because of his welfare program. Stories were circulated that the National Broadcasting Company had put up the $20,000 and that Catholic Charities had masterminded a complex operation to trap Mitchell.

The opinion expressed by a letter writer to *The Cincinnati Enquirer* was typical of that of many strong pro-Mitchellites: "Another American who had the courage to oppose the big spenders and the do-gooders is being given the old smear treatment . . . he [Mitchell] takes his place along side of Lindberg, Dies, Coughlin, MacArthur, McCarthy, and Walker."

Mitchell claimed he had received hundreds of letters, including some from persons "in high places," which expressed belief in his innocence. He declined to reveal the names of the senders or give a more specific figure on the number of writers. His supporters, however, Mitchell was unhappy to learn, were more willing to sign their names to a letter than a check. A week after his arrest, the City Manager tried to persuade a top official of the Citizens for Solvent Government—created to support his welfare program —to use the organization to collect funds to pay for his trial. He was turned down.

Letters sent by Mitchell to his supporters throughout the country indicating his need for funds, netted him less than $100. He was forced to borrow $8,000 from his mother and another $2,000 from his brothers and sisters to help pay for his defense attorneys.

Mitchell's more fervid backers may have maintained their trust in him, but it would be misleading to suggest that the City Manager's standing in the community and in the nation had not been weakened by his arrest. (The surest indication that Mitchell had fallen back into the ranks of the ordinary citizen came when he returned to Newburgh after being booked and found a ticket on his car, parked overnight outside City Hall.)

One practical result of the action was to render him politically powerless. Two days after his arrest Mitchell was forced to suspend himself as city manager without pay. Even before his indictment, the ICMA, whose displeasure with Mitchell's actions of the previous year had abated very little, suspended his membership indefinitely.

Newburghers, including some of his supporters, were predicting that, regardless of the outcome of the trial, Mitchell would never again return to City Hall. For it is a popular belief among the masses that all politicians and holders of public office are as crooked as a Catskill stream. (Indeed, one of the Newburgh councilmen was heard to remark after hearing of Mitchell's arrest: "I don't care if he is guilty. It's not city money.") In the eyes of many, the City Manager would be thought guilty regardless of any innocent verdict which might be rendered by a jury. Certainly, it was argued, his association with DeMasi had tainted him.

Mitchell still had many loyal backers, but their number was far fewer than at the height of the welfare controversy. In the local community best estimates were that opinion was about equally divided. Of greater concern to the City Manager was that most of Newburgh's power structure—the lawyers, Republican committeemen, and influential businessmen—had deserted to the anti-Mitchell camp.

After nearly four months of legal maneuvering by defense lawyers for Mitchell and DeMasi, the trial finally began on March 25, 1963, the City Manager's 41st birthday. Mitchell's controversial welfare policy was not legally an issue at the trial, but the defense[2] tried to implant the idea that

[2] Mitchell hired and fired defense lawyers like a desperate baseball manager bringing in relief pitchers during a close game. He began with the services of two New York City criminal lawyers, William Kleinman and Eugene Gold. On March 4, when the trial was originally scheduled to start, he informed the court he had discharged them because their fee, which he later put at $30,000, was too high.

At the recommendation of a Texas acquaintance, he hired Edward M. Chapman, a 70-year-old retired New York City Housing Court judge. After one week of trial, Mitchell discharged Chapman and hired DeMasi's attorney, William Power Maloney, a vigorous and aggressive defender. Maloney was the winning attorney. He later was forced to obtain a court judgement against Mitchell in an effort to obtain a $10,000 fee he said the City Manager owed him for his services.

Maloney was to become better known a little more than a year later as the attorney for the kidnapped gangland leader Joseph (Joe Bananas) Bonanno. The gangster, according to news stories, was taken by force from in front of Maloney's apartment where he was to spend the night.

It was another bit of irony that Mitchell should be defended by one of the criminal lawyers he had charged with marching "toward the omnipotent state of Karl Marx."

the Wahrhaftigs had plotted to frame the City Manager because of the brothers' disagreement with the thirteen points. Questioned on the witness stand, the brothers said they had no opinion on the welfare controversy.

Mitchell's trial drew reporters from all the New York metropolitan newspapers and the wire services. Television cameramen and radio reporters appeared intermittently for taped interviews and flocked to the courtroom when the verdict was announced.

The City Manager characteristically appeared to bask in all the publicity. "I shall stand before the bar of justice in the historic footprints of the lowly, the average and the great," he said in a statement just before the trial. He invited all community residents to his trial and later asked the acting city manager to free as many city employees as possible from their duties so they could attend. The request was not granted.

During recesses in the trial, Mitchell welcomed personally all local residents, often introducing them to each other in the corridor outside the courtroom. I drove him back from the Court House to his hotel late one afternoon. In the back seat of the car Mitchell looked through the afternoon newspapers for an account of the trial. He seemed affronted if a newspaper had no story on the courtroom battle.

Nevertheless, Mitchell's post-trial statements indicate he was more worried about the outcome than he led courtroom spectators to believe. Manhattan's Bowery is not far from the criminal courts building and Mitchell revealed that during the days the trial was held he often took walks around the area. "I used to see these bums on the street and I wondered 'is this what happens to you? Is this what will happen to me?'" he confided.

Mitchell's underlying worries may have prompted him

to make a senseless denouncement of the prosecution mid-
way in the trial. His attack was in the form of a typewritten
statement released to the press accusing Hogan's office of
using methods "reminiscent of Nazi Germany."

"Since the arrest, I've heard that the DA's office has had
teams here [in Newburgh] peeking at bank accounts, in-
quiring at bars and hotels and using other dirty methods."
The "dirty methods" used by the district attorney's office
uncovered a mass of circumstantial evidence, but the case
was far from being ironclad. For one thing, the detectives
had not directly connected Mitchell with the $20,000. An
obvious method would have been to trail DeMasi after he
received the cash to his supposed meeting with Mitchell.
But detectives said outside of the courtroom this course was
discussed and abandoned because they were afraid of losing
DeMasi's car in heavily falling snow.

The prosecution, headed by Assistant District Attorney
Grebow did, however, have a signed confession from De-
Masi in which he contended the $20,000 was to have been
given to Mitchell in McKneally's office on December 7. But
the confession could be admitted as evidence only against
the pudgy, forty-two-year-old real estate agent. Mitchell admitted referring DeMasi to the Wahrhaftigs, but denied
asking him to collect a $20,000 bribe. Extraordinarily calm
and unshaken during his three days on the witness stand, the
City Manager said that he regarded DeMasi as a "de-
veloper."

Despite evidence that fourteen telephone calls had been
made between Mitchell's office and DeMasi during the
month before their arrest, Mitchell's deliberate, quiet-voiced
manner of parrying the prosecution's questions helped raise
doubts about his guilt in the minds of many of the jurors.

Recordings of conversations between DeMasi and the

Wahrhaftigs in which the loquacious go-between declared the $20,000 was for Mitchell and members of the City Council were presented to the jury. A recording of a December 4 call in which Mitchell talked to Stephen Wahrhaftig was inconclusive. In it the City Manager was heard saying of DeMasi, "I've never gone all the way with him like we're going this time." Newburgh's administrative head explained to the jury he was talking about a housing development.

The final bit of evidence presented against Mitchell was circumstantial and had only a tenuous tie-in with the alleged crime. Nevertheless, it was the only piece of evidence which caused the City Manager's face to redden in embarrassment. It was an order, placed with a Newburgh auto dealer three days before Mitchell's arrest, for an air-conditioned $7,107 Lincoln Continental in Presidential black. The car was to have been delivered on Christmas.

There are some who interpret Mitchell's choice of Presidential black as symbolic of the City Manager's ultimate ambitions. The interpretation is perhaps far-fetched. Nevertheless, Mitchell's desire to exchange a salmon Chrysler convertible for an ebony, air-conditioned Lincoln represented a subtle change in personality since he became a national figure. He was still inclined toward ostentation. But the youthful dazzle had been replaced by a middle-aged desire to display wealth and an exalted position in society.

Mitchell once confided to me that it was a car which first caused him to realize his family didn't belong living in Chevy Chase. "I was friendly with a girl my own age in the neighborhood," he said, reminiscing in his office. "I remember one Christmas she invited me over to her house. When I got there, her present from her father, a new convertible, wrapped in celophane and tied with a red ribbon was in the driveway. When you're a kid you don't forget those things. I realized then that we didn't belong in the neighborhood."

Perhaps Mitchell's intended Christmas present to himself was a 25-year-old wish to prove that he did indeed belong in the neighborhood. As a display of wealth, however, the Lincoln Continental would have been egregiously misleading. Grebow disclosed that at the time the City Manager ordered the car, he had only $498 in his bank account, was paying a $22,000 mortgage on his home, a $1,600 bank loan, and his son's tuition at a small, private college in Poughkeepsie. In explaining his intended purchase, Mitchell told the court that with the trade-in of his 1957 convertible the price of the Lincoln would have been cut by the dealer to $5,296. Of the sum, he testified, $4,000 would have been paid through a bank loan. For a man who had the responsibility of balancing a city budget, Mitchell's personal finances were tangled and reckless.

Following a trial which lasted nearly a month, the jury began deliberating at 12:08 P.M. on Monday, April 22. Members of the panel were as divided over the question of Mitchell's guilt as the public. At 5:57 P.M. the jury returned to announce it could not agree on a decision. It was sent back, with a crisp lecture on its duty to determine the outcome of the case, by state Supreme Court Justice Joseph A. Sarafite, who had presided over the trial with a firm hand.

There was no decision that night or the next morning and reporters were saying to each other that it looked like a hung jury. Behind the closed doors in the jury room, members of the panel revealed later, the issue was deadlocked, 5 to 5, with two members undecided.

"There was a hard core of four jurors who said from the start that they would not convict Mitchell. There was a hard core of four who insisted from the start that Mitchell was guilty," one of the jurors told Milton Lewis of *The New York Herald Tribune*.

At 4:10 P.M. Tuesday the hard core which thought Mitchell guilty suddenly gave in. "I was afraid that Judge Sarafite would keep us locked up for a week," one member confided. "So we fell back on those two little words, 'reasonable doubt.' "

The jurors were able to convince themselves of a reasonable doubt on two points: The money was never turned over to Mitchell; and nowhere in the testimony of the Wahrhaftigs was Mitchell quoted as demanding $20,000. (Stephen Wahrhaftig said that Mitchell had held a slip of paper before him on which the number twenty was written, but the City Manager denied in court that the figure referred to $20,000.)

There was little excitement among newsmen and spectators when the jurors returned to the courtroom at 4:10 P.M. Mitchell and DeMasi looked mildly interested. Most of those present had been waiting since Monday for a verdict. Five times before the jury had filed solemnly into the wood-paneled courtroom on the thirteenth floor of the New York City Criminal Courts Building. Four times it had asked for additional information. The other occasion had been when the foreman announced it was deadlocked. There was no reason to suspect a verdict had been reached this time.

As the eleven men and one woman were seated, Mitchell and DeMasi stood up perfunctorily and faced the jury. A questioning look appeared on Mitchell's otherwise expressionless face when jury foreman Wendell P. Moore announced a verdict had been reached. DeMasi looked tense and worried.

Three times the clerk of the court read one of the charges against Mitchell. Each time Moore replied in a low voice

that the jury found the defendant "not guilty." When the
third and last "not guilty" was proclaimed, Mitchell breathed
a sigh of relief which could be heard throughout the courtroom. It was the only indication of any emotion the City
Manager allowed himself. His face was expressionless.

Because of the nature of the charge both DeMasi and
Mitchell had to be found guilty, or both had to be declared
innocent. It was only a formality for the clerk to read the
charges against DeMasi and for Moore to repeat the words
"not guilty."[3]

One member of the Mitchell jury told a reporter that one
of the reasons why those who thought the City Manager
guilty were willing to vote for his acquittal was because they
felt that his reputation and career as a city official had been
damaged by the arrest and trial. Indeed, Mitchell appeared
in serious difficulty when he returned to Newburgh as city
manager. The chairman of the City Republican Committee
asked for his ouster; the Newburgh *Evening News* editorialized, "Mr. Mitchell has outlived his usefulness in the
community." The county's other daily, the *Middletown
Times-Herald Record,* asked the City Manager to leave the
community. A poll conducted by the local radio station disclosed that of the 499 city residents writing in, 74 per cent
felt Mitchell should not be retained. Two community organizations, the Greater Newburgh Action Committee and
the Greater Newburgh Community Council, asked for his
resignation.

Yet letters to the editor of *The Evening News* disclosed
that Mitchell still had strong support among much of the

---

[3] DeMasi's troubles, however, were not over. As soon as he
stepped outside the courtroom he was rearrested by Hogan's men on
a charge of grand larceny involving the $20,000. A New York grand
jury later failed to indict him and the case was dropped.

citizenry. The local Gold Star mothers sent a cake to his house. Congratulatory letters and telegrams poured in from all parts of the country. Nevertheless, local Republican officials had come to regard the City Manager as a political liability. In May both major parties named candidates for the council who were pledged to oust Mitchell from office if elected. Behind the scene, Councilmen McIntyre and Green urged him to resign.

On July 8 he submitted his resignation, effective in early October. As he did, he revealed his intention to become an organizer for the John Birch Society. Mitchell said,

> The Society is growing. It has prominent and respectable people working for it. They fight communism, and I feel that is a fine thing.
>
> In my opinion they are the true moderates. They follow a reasonable course in public affairs. They are opposing the socialistic trend which is taking place.

On the same day Councilman McKneally, who did not receive Republican endorsement for reelection, announced he would not run again. "You have seen the passing of an era," he said, referring to the day's announcements. "Right or wrong, we were the most colorful, controversial administration in [local] history."

Those who thought Mitchell's philosophies and talents were ideally fitted for office in the Birch Society were surprised when on July 25 Mitchell announced he had changed his mind about working for the organization. The "true moderates" of three weeks before, he indicated, had now become too extreme for his satisfaction.

"While I am in agreement with many of the principles espoused by the society," he said in a prepared press release, "I find that my own background in government leaves me in a far more moderate position."

The Birchers, Mitchell told me that day in a conversation in his office, "believe that the Kremlin is behind everyone who believes in big government. I just don't go that far. The politicians don't need the Kremlin." Apathy on the part of the public and the tendency of politicians to enlarge their power, he said, was creating oppressive big government.

There was a more personal reason for Mitchell's discontent with the society. It may have been the major cause for the termination of his brief association with the organization. "Once you join this group," he told me, "it's like joining a monastery. They want to OK every word you say. I'm a kind of person who's always spoken his mind." Mitchell had been dealing directly with Robert Welch, the inflexible head and founder of the right-wing society. The organization was just too small for two men of such strong opinions.

Unfortunately for the outgoing City Manager, the political atmosphere which prompted his resignation had not changed. The resignation could not be retracted. On September 6 Mitchell, still jobless, left City Hall for the last time as city manager. There were no farewell dinners.

"Good riddance," George McKneally, the man most responsible for bringing Mitchell to Newburgh and his staunchest "friend" on the council, told the press. "The city is fortunate to be rid of Mitchell and his problems."

Most people predicted that Mitchell would never again be appointed to a political office. After seeking manager appointments without success for nearly a year, in mid-1964 he accepted the post of national field director for the segregationist Citizens Councils of America with the ludicrous results which have been footnoted.

Those who counted him out of political life—at least north of the Mason–Dixon Line—were wrong, however. In August 1965 he was appointed city manager by the seven members of the non-partisan City Council of Hollidaysburg, Pennsylvania, a white, upper-class suburb of Altoona, one-sixth the size of Newburgh. It has no welfare problems. In February 1966 a reporter for the *Altoona Mirror*, Sandra Ivory, described him as a man intent in keeping things moving in the community. His salary, substantially lower than at Newburgh, had been raised $600 to $8,659.

It's doubtful that Mitchell's dream of one day being in Washington has been shattered. It lies dormant awaiting only a popular issue, the applause of an audience, and a banner headline to make it bright again.

THE NEWBURGH NEGRO MINISTER, the Rev. William D.
Burton, once characterized the city's welfare controversy as
"a pregnant mountain that gave birth to a panicky mouse."
The accuracy of this colorful description can be seen when
the results of the initially acclaimed welfare crusade are
looked at.

In private conversations and public statements, Mitchell
boasted that the Newburgh program would (not necessarily
in the order of importance):

1. Cut the number of persons on relief.
2. Relieve the taxpayer's burden.
3. Stem the immigration of southern migrants (Negroes).
4. Halt the decay of the city.
5. Result in greater local control of the welfare department.
6. Be adopted by other local and state governments.
7. Influence the policy of the federal government.
8. Put able-bodied reliefers to work.
9. Disclose a great number of legal and moral chiselers.
10. Promote Newburgh as a desirable place in which to
live and locate industry.

The program produced several unexpected results, but

not the ones of which the City Manager boasted, as we shall see later in this chapter.

As late as August 1962, eight months after the court had permanently enjoined the city from carrying out twelve of its thirteen points, Mitchell told a *New York Times* reporter that despite state "interference" and the court injunctions "we have succeeded in effecting our welfare reforms." "I've relied on new men, not new regulations."[1]

One of these men was a former policeman hired as a part-time investigator to check on the activities of welfare recipients at irregular intervals and hours. Another was a business administration graduate promoted from caseworker to intake supervisor to screen applicants for welfare. Mitchell boasted he was trimming welfare costs through "careful replacement of soft, motherly, university-trained social workers with hard-boiled, tough-minded people to handle the case load."

State welfare officials expressed concern about the methods used to discourage applicants. "To harass, to threaten, to frighten, to punish—these are the elements of the Newburgh plan in practice," State Commissioner of Social Welfare Raymond W. Houston said.

"Fear to apply for relief has settled into the minds of many persons in need. They are afraid to be held up to public shame and realize that they are going to be handled unsympathetically," Mayor Ryan declared in a speech to a labor union audience in Chicago in May 1962.

The program of harassment probably had its greatest effect on the fearful minds of many of the aged. Mrs. Helen Doulin, a caseworker, related in late 1961:

Some of our old age clients . . . in spite of our telling them

[1] *New York Times,* August 20, 1962.

differently, insist upon coming to the office once a month.
These old folks do not have the money for taxi fare, and
many of them walk many, many blocks, because at one
time or another, they read in the paper that once a month
cases must report to the office. This is where the psychological warfare, to my way of feeling, is doing the greatest
harm.

Following an investigation, the state Department of Welfare released a report in March 1962 charging that local
welfare officials had arbitrarily denied relief to some applicants and used pressures to keep needy persons off the rolls.
"Intake interviews are conducted in an atmosphere of pressure, and the method of questioning disturbs and confuses
the applicant," the report found.

The type of pressure to which the department was referring was illustrated by a woman writer, Fern Eckman, who
described the experiences of a 23-year-old girl when she
asked Bert Grenis, Mitchell's hand-picked intake supervisor
for assistance. Miss Eckman, in a *Redbook Magazine* article, quoted the girl as saying of Grenis:

> He screamed at me, "Don't you know when you come here
> and ask for money that you're asking the taxpayer for
> money?" I tried to tell him that I was a taxpayer too. When
> he screamed at me that way, I felt—I felt small. That was
> the first time I'd ever asked for help. I felt, was I doing the
> wrong thing? He was so nasty I started to cry. . . .
> She fled. Eviction was inevitable. . . .

In its report the state found that of the thirty-four families denied relief in December 1961 "sixteen appeared to
have been arbitrarily denied with little consideration having
been given to the needs of the applicant, and another five

were borderline and probably should have been assigned to a caseworker for investigation." In one of the half dozen instances in which state investigators visited the homes of persons denied relief they found that the family had to be broken up, with the children being cared for by relatives because the parents had no means of caring for them.

In terms of human misery and shame the Newburgh program may have been costly. But that is not its most vulnerable point. Shame and want suffered by a nameless few do not trouble the taxpayer who is unaware of and unwilling to believe there may be victims of welfare policies which purport to save him money. The principal argument Mitchell and other advocates of the Newburgh approach used to justify the program is one on which it is most defenseless—the theme of economy.

In late 1961 and throughout 1962, Mitchell, in speeches across the country, made much of the fact that he had reduced the city's 1962 taxes. The resultant saving to the taxpayer, he claimed, was due to his crackdown on welfare payments. In fact, the reduction was extremely small, almost inconsequential. It amounted to a nickel per $1,000 of assessed valuation. It is significant that Mitchell never mentioned the amount of his tax reduction to out-of-state audiences.

Even that very small decrease was due partly to a cut in other budget items and to deficit spending—for which taxpayers were to pay later. Snow removal, which cost $140,-000 the previous year, was budgeted at $24,000; the police pension fund was cut by $19,500; street and recreation budgets were reduced by $10,000 each; health and public services were cut by $8,000. These cuts were not sufficient. A state audit of the city's finances showed Mitchell used

$130,000 of nonexistent cash surpluses to balance the budget. Without the imaginary windfall the tax rate would have been increased by $2.50.[2]

Mitchell claimed his tax cut was due almost entirely to a $92,485 reduction in the welfare budget. In fact, welfare costs rose in 1961—the year of the thirteen points—and rose again in 1962, 1963, and 1964, and were still rising in 1965.[3]

Figures from the city's welfare department show it spent $13,283 more for relief in 1961 than in the previous year.[4] Part of the reason for the increase was the establishment of two new programs by the state and federal governments— temporary aid to dependent children and medical aid to the aged. The new programs were accompanied by a rise in the cost of several categories of aid, principally aid to dependent children, which rose 15 per cent, and in an increase in administrative costs because of the addition of two (philosophically tested) caseworkers and a special investigator.

A 1962 report released by New York State Comptroller Arthur Levitt disclosed that in the previous year of welfare controversy Newburgh paid almost six times as much in local taxes for welfare as residents of Beacon, Newburgh's sister city across the river. Compared with the other six cities in the state which operate their own welfare districts,

[2] *Middletown Times-Herald & Record,* Janaury 22, 1963.

[3] The 1965 welfare budget was nearly one and one-half million dollars, which is a half million more than when Mitchell began his program.

[4] When the $5,000 in legal fees Newburgh paid to Hirschberg, the salary of an extra secretary to answer Mitchell's fan mail, and the expenses of the City Manager in spreading his welfare gospel across the country are considered, the increase is nearly doubled.

Newburgh was second highest in *per capita* welfare payments.[5]

Despite the headlines and the acclaim, Newburgh's expenditures for welfare were 7.1 per cent higher the last full year Mitchell served as city manager (1962) than the year before he began his crusade (1960). During the same period the number of persons on public assistance went up 3.26 per cent.[6]

Early in 1964 Mitchell's successor as city manager asked for a ten-year breakdown of the costs of welfare assistance, excluding burial and administrative expenses and costs of running the City Home and Infirmary. The figures disclosed public assistance payments in Newburgh rose from $428,-738.92 in 1954 to $570,478.77 in the pre-Mitchell year of 1960. In 1961 they rose to $583,278.92, increased to $596,469.37 in 1962, and leaped to $768,477.76 in 1963. At the end of 1964 they had almost doubled the 1961 figure, reaching just under a million dollars.

It's true that Mitchell has been gone from Newburgh since the middle of 1963 and no attempt has been made by his successor or the present City Council to continue his tactics. Nevertheless, despite denial of relief to some destitute applicants and harassment of those receiving welfare payments, Mitchell was never able to stop welfare costs from rising while he was in power.

[5] First was Binghamton with a *per capita* cost of $16.00. Newburgh residents paid an average of $13.70 each in city taxes to welfare. Poughkeepsie, twenty miles north of Newburgh on the opposite shore, had a *per capita* cost of $13.05. Lowest was Auburn with a *per capita* payment of $10.03. In Beacon, which is part of a county welfare district, residents paid only an average of $2.61 each for welfare.

[6] Newburgh *Evening News,* July 18, 1963.

In April 1965, 1,439 persons were on the city welfare rolls, a third more than when Mitchell ordered the welfare muster during the same month four years earlier.

Ironically, Newburgh's attempted crackdown on welfare recipients may have had a reverse effect. In March 1964 city Welfare Commissioner Petrillo stated it was his belief that the sharper rise in welfare payments in 1962 and 1963 was due partly to all the publicity welfare received in the city. According to the commissioner, many persons did not realize they could get the meager help offered by the public until the welfare controversy.

Many supporters of Newburgh's severe welfare proposals argue that if the state court had allowed the city to keep its thirteen points in effect a sharp drop in the number of welfare recipients and costs would have taken place without creating hardship to needy children or the aged. A look at Newburgh's 1961 welfare statistics belies that notion. If in July 1961 when Mitchell put the thirteen points into operation, aid had been denied to every adult on relief not disabled, blind, or aged, he would have cut the number of the 915 persons then on welfare by only 14 per cent.

The amount of money he would have saved the local taxpayer is even smaller. As mentioned in Chapter 8, of the 128 able-bodied adults under sixty-five receiving relief payments, most were mothers receiving aid to dependent children for support of their families. Since the city's share of the ADC cost was only 18 per cent, the effect on the local taxpayer would have been insignificant.

If every man, woman and child in the ADC and general (home) relief programs—the ones at which Newburgh's program was aimed—had been denied relief in 1961, the city would have saved $60,000, or about $2 per inhabitant.

Many of the costs to the community because of the failure of its welfare program could not be determined simply by a look at the city's welfare budget or its tax rate—the Newburgh tax rate nearly doubled in three years, from a $30.95 rate in 1962 to a $52 rate in 1965, due in large measure to the deferred spending policy Mitchell adopted to enable him to show a token tax cut despite rising costs. Officials of the city's only hospital became so concerned with what they claimed was an increasing number of payment denials by the welfare department that in 1962 a full-time social worker was added to the hospital staff. An important part of his job was to make certain the hospital received the fullest financial help permitted by law for its care of welfare patients.

As we talked in his office a rainy spring day in late April of 1964, Commissioner Petrillo expressed bitterness that the previous City Council had cut the welfare budget for hospital care from $50,000 in 1961 to $30,000 annually in the following two years. The cut was made despite increasing hospital costs. "How are you going to stop people from getting sick?" he asked.

Denial of medical payments to hospitalized welfare patients may look like a savings to the taxpayer when the city's welfare budget is published. But the costs of welfare hospitalization and medical care has to be paid by someone and if it is not shared by the community, the expense usually shows up in unseen charges in a paying patient's hospital bill.

The local Catholic Charities office, the only private community agency providing substantial material help to the poor, experienced a doubling in the number of families seeking aid since the start of the welfare battle. According to Dan Boudreau, the average number of applications for

material aid in the years 1959 and 1960 was fifteen
monthly. In the following three years, he reported, the average jumped to more than thirty monthly. The increase resulted in the hiring of an additional caseworker and a rise
of 75 per cent in the bureau's budget.

Boudreau attributes the increase in the number of applications partly to Catholic Charities' role in battling the
Newburgh welfare code. More local persons are aware of
its services than before, he believes. He also blames the
city welfare department. He claims many persons have had
to be cared for by Catholic Charities after having been
denied local aid. (A similar result of private charities and
hospitals having to increase their budgets because of a
tight welfare policy is reported in a 1963 study[7] done in
Clermont County, Ohio in which poor-relief funds were
sharply curtailed in 1961 following defeat of a proposed
local tax levy for welfare aid. The study, by the Community
Health and Welfare Council of the Greater Cincinnati Area,
found "that in some form the community paid and is still
paying the bill for most of these cases [denied relief]
since the needs of the families and children for help have
continued. The burden has shifted from public resources to
landlords, grocers and physicians, to churches, civic groups,
voluntary agencies, schools and individuals such as friends
and relatives.")

If any of the scores of newsmen were to return to the
Hudson River city they helped make famous they would
discover how little Mitchell succeeded in changing its

[7] *Effect on Families and Individuals in a Rural Community When
Poor Relief was Exhausted: A Study of 162 Cases in Clermont
County, Ohio Whose Total Poor Relief Grants Were Discontinued,*
Department of Health, Education, and Welfare.

welfare operations. The requirement that all able-bodied welfare recipients pick up their checks at the welfare departments was dropped early in 1962. Work relief was finally started in August of 1961, when a thirty-seven-year-old white laborer with a long history of being on welfare was given a job sweeping the City Hall floors.

It has sputtered through the following years without fanfare. The average number of work reliefers has been two or three a month, with periods of a month or more without anyone on work relief. The high mark was reached in March 1962 when nineteen unemployed men were put to work painting the City Home for the Aged.[8]

In May 1965 five work reliefers were employed by the city. They were paid the state minimum of $1.25 hourly.

Most of the women receiving relief in the city, Mr. Petrillo told a reporter in an interview,[9] are middle-aged or elderly and, if they are able-bodied, are employed part time as domestics and babysitters. Even so, he said, they didn't make enough money to pay for their basic needs. The Welfare Commissioner[10] also found that supervision was so bothersome and costly it hardly paid to have only a few persons on work relief. The practice of photographing welfare recipients was abandoned soon after it was started.

The caseworkers in the department who opposed Mitchell and his program tell of a blunder when adult reliefers were being photographed which amuses them. It seems the

[8] In comparison, the pre-Mitchell era high was twenty-five work reliefers employed at one time.

[9] Newburgh *Evening News,* July 2, 1962.

[10] Petrillo was fired from his $8,085 post in late November, 1964. Two weeks later he was hired as deputy welfare commissioner by a three to two vote of the City Council.

photographer forgot to write the name and identifying number of many of the welfare recipients when he took their picture. The result is there are a number of photos of unidentified reliefers in the files.

None of the city's new procedures such as the photographing requirement or the hiring of a special investigator uncovered a single case of a recipient receiving aid illegally. In early 1962 though, the department learned of a fifty-one-year-old woman who signed an application for financial aid for two children not her own. She was never admitted to the welfare rolls. Later, after pleading guilty to attempting to extort funds from the Newburgh Welfare Department, she was sentenced to sixty days in jail.

One of the many ironies about the Newburgh controversy is that the city, which was depicted in 1961 as leading a revolt against staid and flaccid welfare policies, could in the mid-sixties be used as an example of a community which remained rooted to policies of more than a decade before. At the same time other communities were experimenting with new procedures in an effort to reduce welfare rolls.

For example, in 1965 fifty-three of the sixty-five local welfare departments in the state were distributing federal surplus foods to welfare and other low income families. Most of them had been taking advantage of the program for more than three years. Newburgh still had made no effort to make use of the plan.

St. Paul, Minnesota, reports impressive results in curbing juvenile delinquency among welfare families and dropping one-sixth of its welfare families from the rolls within six months. It did this by concentrating the efforts of its social workers on the families which it felt could be helped through intensive guidance. The aged, the mentally deficient, and others judged unemployable were given routine financial aid. Without adding social workers caseloads were reduced to thirty each.

Chicago has a program to train illiterates on the welfare rolls to read and write and to train others in needed occupations. Programs similar to the ones in Chicago and St. Paul had been tried with successful results in Washington, D.C., Florida, Pennsylvania, Indiana, and other states. In Denver the welfare department established an incentive budgeting system which permits an ADC mother to keep $25 of earned income without losing any welfare payments, plus a quarter of everything she earns over $25.

None of these practices had been tried in Newburgh.

Welfare officials in some New York county welfare districts report they have shaved costs by establishing a ceiling on the amount of rent which will be paid. Although Petrillo predicted in 1964 that rising rents would greatly contribute to forcing the welfare budget to a record high, a rent ceiling was not suggested.

New York State for several years has had a program designed to teach ADC mothers how to do household chores efficiently, care for their children, and plan for the family's future needs, through the guidance of a trained social worker. Although the program is 100 per cent reimbursed by the state, and Petrillo believed it was an important first step in keeping future generations off welfare, it had not been instituted in Newburgh. The Commissioner blamed the City Council who failed to include a sum for the program, even though every penny would be returned by the state.

There has been one morale-boosting improvement. Caseworkers' salaries have been raised from a maximum of

$4,500 to one of $5,445. But caseloads still average between seventy and ninety (about state average), and because
of a high turnover, the department has seldom been fully
staffed.

One of the surprising changes has been in the attitude of
Petrillo. Although hired as a man philosophically attuned
to the thinking of Mr. Mitchell, the soft-spoken welfare
official in the intervening years has come to accept many of
the same beliefs held by his predecessor, and by Mitchell's
"soft, motherly, university-trained social workers."[11] Commissioner Petrillo told me during our April 1964 discussion,

> In order to rehabilitate a person you first have to make
> him feel important. Once you motivate the individual then
> you can start fighting the problems. But how can you mo-
> tivate, if you haven't anything to offer? You can't just
> order him to go out and find a job. You can't teach a
> mother to keep a clean house in a rat-infested, ramshackle
> apartment building with broken or boarded-up windows.
> You have to change the environment. I wish I could take
> the council down to some of these places.

Because welfare is principally connected with slums, with
unemployment, failure, broken homes, illness, loneliness,
hardship, and all the other unpleasant aspects of modern
civilization, the proud natives and long-time residents of the

---

[11] In September 1962 only a few months after Mitchell had made
this statement he told a state commission investigating welfare as a
result of the Newburgh controversy, "I recognize the dedication of
those in the welfare field. I salute their sincerity; I sympathize with
their problems; I understand the complexities facing them. The
many barbs and darts hurled at these public servants as a group,
such as 'do-gooders,' 'bleeding hearts,' and similar epithets, are
undeserved, and show a callous misunderstanding of the problems
extant in welfare today."

city fear that too many negative aspects of their community
have been exposed to the unsympathetic eye of the nation.
It can be argued that from their point of view, they are
right. Certainly, the publicity has brought no new industries
to the community. In fact, the period following the out-
break of the controversy marked a drop in Newburgh's total
real estate valuation for the first time in its history. In 1961
the valuation was its peak of $56,884,989. The following
year it dropped to $56,686,482. By 1965 it had dropped
another four million dollars to $52,796,063.

An urban renewal project for which plans were filed with
the Federal Government in 1957 was bogged down in early
1966 over the question of where a public housing unit
should be located. And an area for the site at which demo-
lition had started in late 1961 was overgrown with weeds.

There's not much talk of welfare in public places around
Newburgh anymore. There is an attitude that too much has
been said and written and above all, televised, about the
city and its welfare program. The community would like to
forget about that chapter in its history and live down its
reputation as a welfare city.

Newburgh's outspoken School Superintendent Dr. Harold
Monson observed as we talked in his office four years after
the welfare muster:

> Mitchell was a passing storm. He halted things for a while.
> He gave people a reason for not doing anything. Mitchell
> set everything back while he was here. He was a figure
> around which the negative and the do-nothing element in
> the community rallied. In the meantime property values
> worsened and the community made no effort to improve
> anything. But when Mitchell showed he didn't have any-
> thing to offer, the thinking citizen discovered that something

had to be done. Mitchell remains a negative influence in the sense he solidified the opposition to the poor and the Negro and so has made integration harder.

However, the ferment produced some positive results worth noting. Many citizens began to look more closely at their community and its deterioration. Organizations composed of businessmen, professional people, and other leading citizens, such as the Greater Newburgh Action Committee and the Greater Area Industrial Developers Corporation sprang up. Their purpose was to bring new industry to the community, instill new vigor into the city's moribund business life, and impart new civic awareness to its citizens. It is too early to determine whether they will achieve success.

Led by Rev. Frank Jones and Superintendent Monson and encouraged by a sympathetic city administration, the Newburgh Community Action Committee took advantage of war-on-poverty funds to establish Project Head-Start and Neighborhood Youth Corps programs in the summer of 1965. Most of the preschool youngsters and a heavy percentage of the teenagers were from Mitchell's "welfare wards." Further requests for federal money were planned by the 33-year-old Negro minister for such community action projects as a homemaking program, a day nursery, adult classes in reading and writing, home management, family financial counseling, neighborhood centers, and a housing information center.

On January 1, 1966, the Newburgh welfare district finally was absorbed into the county district, thus ending the city's struggle with increasing welfare loads and rising relief budgets. "It's one of the greatest things which has happened to Newburgh in some time," a councilman asserted when the agreement was reached. Some 1,400 persons remained on the relief rolls at the time. There was no work-relief program.

The controversy also awakened some residents, both Negro and white, to the need of more communication and cooperation between the races. One of the first acts of the new administration was to appoint a Human Relations Committee of whites and Negroes to look into the questions of poor housing, education, and employment.

For, like many of the other objectives of the welfare program, the administration's aim to curb the influx of Negro families was not achieved. The number of Negro children in Newburgh schools has been increasing steadily throughout the sixties. In 1961 two Newburgh elementary schools were predominantly Negro. In 1965 the number had increased to four.

Rev. William Burton has admitted an average of one hundred new persons into his church—most of them newcomers to the city—in each year from 1961 to 1966. In comparison, eighty new members were admitted in 1960. He and other Negro leaders say Negro families are arriving at the same rate as before the welfare crisis. "There is a constant flux, but certainly more are coming than leaving," he observed.

At the city's polls the welfare controversy and Mitchell became a handicap for the councilmen who had brought the impulsive City Manager to Newburgh. In 1961 Councilman Doulin and McIntyre, running on what Mitchell termed a "mandate" for the welfare program, received only 52 per cent of the vote against two relatively unknown Democratic businessmen. A different decision by two hundred voters would have given the Democrats a majority and halted the welfare program then being observed closely by an interested and largely favorable press.

Two years later, for the first time in the city's history, the Democrats gained control of the council, winning the post of mayor (Mayor Ryan declined to run for re-election) and the two council seats up for grabs. Of the five-member council in office when the thirteen points were drawn up, none was still in office at the beginning of 1966. On the night of the GOP's historic defeat in Newburgh, the city's Republican chairman told a reporter, "I don't think the good Lord could win on the record of this administration."

And out of the ferment, indirectly and vicariously, came much that was good. In a conversation with Mitchell in February 1964 he admitted to me he didn't know of any variations of the Newburgh program which had been adopted by local or state welfare departments. Yet, he looked back on the controversy with a feeling of accomplishment. "I caused those in welfare to take a new look at their programs and I made the politicans understand that there is a feeling in the people against welfare. We gave them something to chew on," he said.

Certainly, the controversy Mitchell stirred up had influence on the varied national welfare programs designed to get recipients off the dole through education and training which were to come into being in the next four years.

Virginia R. Doscher, staff associate for the American Public Welfare Association, wrote me in June 1965,

> I think it is quite obvious that public interest in welfare and the problems of poverty has been steadily growing since the Newburgh incident. Of course, not all of this can be considered a result of Newburgh, but I do think it served to trigger interest where before there had been generally apathy. . . . It seems to be since Newburgh that people have been willing to listen to some of the things that welfare seemed to be able to find only deaf ears for before.

President John F. Kennedy displayed an informed knowledge of the challenges posed by Newburgh when on February 1, 1962, he became the first chief executive to issue a special welfare message to Congress. The late President, in stressing the need for rehabilitation, said that looking on the poverty stricken "with scorn and suspicion is inconsistent with their nearly universal preference to be independent." Without mentioning Newburgh, he declared:

> Communities which have . . . for whatever motives . . . attempted to save money through ruthless cutbacks in their welfare rolls have found their efforts to little avail. The root problems remained. . . .

Even before the President's message, in December 1961 Abraham A. Ribicoff, then Secretary of Health, Education, and Welfare, ordered a ten-point overhauling of the federal program. Included among the ten points were a request that states adopt tighter procedures for detecting and halting welfare fraud, an order requiring states to establish organizations to locate deserting parents of children on relief, and a requirement that states develop a better training program for caseworkers. While denying that the overhauling had been prompted by the strict welfare code adopted in Newburgh, he conceded, "Newburgh may have sensationalized this, and it may have had a salutary effect."

Paul Martin, chief of the Gannett News Service Washington, D.C. Bureau, quoted an official of the Public Assistance Bureau, which administers the federal end of all state and local welfare programs, as saying:

> Newburgh dramatized the situation. It provoked a national reaction. It created a great deal of public discussion. It has caused us to review the matter, and it will cause Congress to give a lot of attention to public welfare.

When I visited Washington in 1962 a top HEW official told me, "There's not a person in Congress that the program hasn't had a psychological effect on."

The Newburgh welfare controversy occurred at a time when Americans were being awakened to the realization that while they were buying electric toothbrushes, color TV sets, backyard swimming pools, power mowers, and motor boats in record numbers, one-fifth of the population—more than 30 million—are without adequate food, housing, clothing, or medical care. One-eighth live in families with incomes which qualify them for relief in their states.

Such books as John Kenneth Galbraith's *The Affluent Society,* Michael Harrington's *The Other America,* Julius Horivitz's *The Inhabitants,* and Ben Bagdikian's *In the Midst of Plenty* had recently been published or were being written to remove the curtains preventing the middle- and upper-class American from seeing the poor. At approximately the same time that Mitchell was ordering the welfare muster, the 1961 Pulitzer Prize was awarded to a Buffalo, New York reporter, Edgar May, for a series of articles on welfare and its recipients in his community. Pope John XXIII's encyclical, *Mater et Magistra* which emphasized the obligation of communities and countries to aid those suffering from poverty, misery, and hunger was issued virtually simultaneously with the Newburgh welfare code. It was a time when some welfare authorities and government officials were beginning to acknowledge shortcomings in policies which did little more than hide the poor from the sight of the average American.

All the great social changes in our nation's history—self-rule, the end of slavery, establishment of public schools, woman's suffrage, the growth of unions, child labor laws, the Social Security Act, civil rights—have had their battlegrounds before becoming accepted as part of American society. Newburgh was the battleground in which clashed white supremacists, Negro organizations, citizens worried over the high cost of government, and citizens concerned over the price of human misery. Mitchell's broadsides at public assistance more often than not missed the target, but their noise helped awaken a nation. A Minnesota public welfare official, L. Irving Peterson, supervisor of Aid to Families with Dependent Children, wrote me:

> There was a special kind of uniqueness about Newburgh that really set it aside. Things have not been the same since. . . . It seems to me that Newburgh focussed attention on responsible governmental leadership and planning. It forced attention to the fact that the welfare of the people is somehow intimately tied to the welfare of the community.

While the battle was continuing federal officials began charting their uncertain new courses designed to strike at the causes, not just the consequences, of poverty—courses intended to prevent and rehabilitate rather than to police and encourage dependence.

A year after the thirteen points went into effect, Congress passed a sweeping welfare reform bill which added $300,000 to the amount to be spent annually by the Federal Government for welfare services. Some of the things the additional money is being used for are the establishment of day-care centers to allow healthy ADC mothers to work, creation of work and training projects aimed at giving the able-bodied needy the ability and desire to support themselves, and for increased federal aid to the aged, blind, and disabled. During the same session, Congress passed the Manpower Development and Training Act under which government funds are provided to train the unemployed and members of poverty-stricken farm families in needed skills such as auto repairing, practical nursing, welding, and typing.

In the two years following President Lyndon B. Johnson's declaration of an "unconditional war on poverty in America" on January 8, 1964, the most far-reaching welfare legislation since the depression became law. The Appalachia Bill was signed authorizing $1 billion in public works projects in the eleven-state region. The Economic Opportunity Act was passed setting up programs to attack poverty and its causes on a variety of fronts. Among the programs established are: A Job Corps to give young men and women sixteen through twenty-one a basic education, training in skills, and work experience; a Neighborhood Youth Corps to provide full- or part-time work for youths of the same age, enabling them to stay in or return to school, or to increase their possibilities for employment; a Work-Study Program to give part-time employment to college students from poor families; Community Action Programs under which up to 90 per cent of the cost of local projects to train, educate, counsel, provide health services for, or otherwise help the poor are paid by the Federal Government; Project Head-Start to prepare deprived preschool children for school; a domestic Peace Corps to work in the slums; loans to low-income farmers and small businessmen; adult education and job training for the needy, including those on relief.

Congress also passed new Social Security amendments providing cheap hospital and nursing home care for the elderly and health care for needy children.

In mid-1965 Joseph Anderson, the executive director of

the National Association of Social Workers, recalled the welfare controversy in a letter to me:

> Four years later the Newburgh crisis seems like a bad dream. If Mr. Mitchell's view had prevailed that welfare rolls were loaded with able-bodied people who should be put to work, Newburgh might have become a rallying point for a return to medieval methods for dealing with the poor. The poor again would have been held accountable alone for their condition and stigmatization, harrassment and punishment, rather than rehabilitation and acceptance of social responsibility, could have been our national course. . . . The Newburgh plan is dead and well buried, but, in the point of time, it served us well as a devil's advocate.

A POSTSCRIPT

THE SAME ISSUE OF *The New York Herald Tribune* which carried a front page announcement of Pope John XXIII's encyclical, *Mater et Magistra,* ran in a nearby column a story on the Newburgh welfare controversy. It is doubtful if many readers saw any connection between the two stories. Yet, each represented a different view of the same theme —man's duty toward his fellow man.

"Essentially the Newburgh crusade is a bold attack upon age-old principles of social justice and neighborly concern for the unfortunate which are our heritage from religion, morality and the fair-play sense of American democracy," Dan Boudreau told a Newburgh audience. "The social doctrine of the Mitchell crusade is that it is a suckers game to spend one's money on the weak element in society."

The evidence displayed during the Newburgh controversy that many good Americans who contribute regularly to their Community Chest, donate their clothing to flood victims, and sponsor Christmas parties for orphans scorn those on relief shocked many welfare officials secure in their semi-private world of forms and statistics. "A large segment of the public despises, even hates the poor," Laurin Hyde, New York City consultant in the managment of health and social services, told members of the National Conference on Social Welfare a year after the beginning of the controversy. "There is the assumption that this is a matter of will. People have willed to be different, to be poor. If we make them, they will change."

This viewpoint was expressed by Mitchell again and again. Without discriminating among them, the needy were "vegetables," or "people whose morality has failed them." Aid to dependent children was "largely the mirror of the sordid part of society." The welfare program was described as being used to finance crime, illegitimacy, disease, and other social evils. Anyone who wanted work could find it. In speeches and statements, he scoffed at the idea that a person could be a victim of his environment. He intimated that welfare recipients were chiefly responsible for the slums in which they lived and for the fires which drove them from their homes.

This picture of welfare recipients is, of course, a distorted and uncharitable one. "Welfare recipients aren't necessarily chisellers, or deadbeats, or criminals. They're poor. They're often ignorant. And in an industrial society, they have a pretty bad time. But they are human beings," former Family Court Judge Edward G. O'Neil of Newburgh observed bravely before television cameras during a documentary seen throughout the nation on the Newburgh controversy.

As the documentary intelligently expressed it, "Social welfare does not cause unemployment. It does not cause lack of education or lack of skill. It does not cause inadequacy of personality or need for medical care. . . ." Welfare does not cause our present problems of automation, the longer life span, increasing mobility of population, or the exodus from central cities to suburbia. It does not contribute to disease, nor is it a factor in tenement fires. And it does not cause slums. All these factors are not caused by welfare. They are the reasons for welfare.

In 1962 Councilman Green, in explaining his reasons for supporting Mitchell, told me:

> You get in city politics and you find you can't replace trucks, you can't pay the police and you can't fix the streets because you haven't got the money. But a lot of money is going out and they tell you this is the welfare budget and it's an open end budget. . . . There are many things which have to be taken care of in the city. We need an incinerator, a sewage treatment plant, a city garage. All these involve millions of dollars. It's obvious something must be done, otherwise essential services won't be performed.

Similar problems beset most American cities as more and more middle- and upper-class taxpayers move out, leaving an increasing percentage of persons who need welfare and other public services but are least able to pay for them. Regardless of the moral questions involved, Mitchell's plan of solving urban blight and cutting the crime rate by harassing and denying the needy could only be successful if, in fact, they were the causes, rather than the victims of the community's problems.

One of the great wrongs of the Newburgh program was that it was a calculated attack upon the human dignity of the welfare recipients. If chiselers are on the rolls, they should be removed. But to subject most of those on public assistance to a muster in which they are on display before a police station, to photograph them as though they were criminals, to label them immoral, to publish their names in the newspaper (as Mitchell suggested) is an offense against the human spirit and against charity. You do not make a person a useful number of society by crushing his self-respect.

In a sermon before his congregation the day after the thirteen points went into effect, the Rev. William Burton preached:

> The most distressing thing about the thirteen point welfare program is not that it discriminates against Negroes.
> . . . The most distressing thing about the plan is that, in a community which professes to be Godly, it stands in bold-faced defiance of the most treasured tenet of our Judeo-Christian tradition, and violates the most basic teaching of both the Old and New Testaments. It violates and mocks the noble concepts of justice, love, and mercy. It is, therefore, not only a salve of selfishness hurled against the weak; it is a sin against God.

Totalitarianism typically begins when a would-be tyrant plays on the anxieties of the majority to begin repressive measures against despised or troublesome minorities. Without being too much of an alarmist, it is not difficult to find parallels between what happened in Germany of the early thirties and what occurred in Newburgh in the early sixties. In both instances a minority, considered inferior in the eyes of members of the society in which it lived, became the scapegoat for many of the misfortunes which were the plague of the times.

"Du bist nichts; dein Volk ist alles" (thou are nothing; the nation is everything), Hitler is supposed to have said. The philosophy is not too different from one expressed by Mitchell: that society has no duty to the individual; the individual's duty is to society. Yet no protest was heard in the community from those who subscribe to the Christian-democratic belief that society has an obligation to all of its individual members. Even Mitchell's political enemies were silent.

"I've wondered how Hitler could have come to power in Germany, a nation which had perhaps the highest ratio of intellectuals in Europe," Mitchell's predecessor, Abrams, told me early in the welfare controversy. "I think I've discovered the answer here in Newburgh. What happens is that the leaders in the community remain silent and let someone like Mitchell take over."

In an interview quoted by Ed May, Mr. Abrams had even deeper insight:

> If I can express your fears, hopes and aspirations so that I can identify myself with your longings and prejudices, then I've got you hooked.
>
> The role of the politician is often one that requires him to express publicly what the people fear privately. Often it's a play-back of their own voices in louder decibels—and that's what happened in Germany and in Newburgh, except in this case the question was to keep the city from going colored.

The prejudice against the welfare recipient which pictures him as a dirty, lazy, able-bodied freeloader, and the anti-Negro feelings which exists in varying degrees in nearly every community in the United States Mitchell was able to exploit for his own ends and ambitions. That is an important lesson and a warning coming from the Newburgh controversy. Mitchell tapped a deep reservoir of popular emotion which extends much further than Newburgh or New York State. Should it be forgotten with its lessons unlearned, then, as seems likely, we will have more Newburghs in the future. For, let's realize, that nothing suggested yet, either by politicians or welfare officials, is going to abolish all welfare programs.

In a society which regards it a sin to cast its aged, its blind, its disabled, its maladjusted, and its incompetent adrift on a convenient ice floe, and which has many members who regard sterilization and artificial birth control as immoral, it is obvious no program or combination of programs is going to return all of those on welfare to useful roles. This presents a problem with which religious leaders, social scientists, welfare workers, politicians, and the public will be struggling for generations.

Too many of us pay no more than lip service to Christ's words:

> When I was thirsty, you gave me something to drink; when I was hungry you gave me to eat; when I was a stranger, you took me in; when I was naked you clothed me; when I was sick and in prison you visited me; because as long as you did it to one of these the least of my brethren, you did it to me.